Baskets Now: USA

Baskets Now: USA

Alan Du Bois
Curator of Decorative Arts

Jack Lenor Larsen
Juror

January 18 - March 10, 2002

Exhibition and Catalogue Sponsors
Robyn and John Horn

Arkansas Arts Center
LITTLE ROCK, ARKANSAS

Publisher:
Arkansas Arts Center
MacArthur Park
Ninth and Commerce Streets
Little Rock, Arkansas 72203-2137
501-372-4000 / 501-375-8053 fax
e-mail: center@arkarts.com

Director and Chief Curator:
Townsend Wolfe

Curator of Art:
Brian Young

Curator of Decorative Arts:
Alan Du Bois

Registrar:
Thom Hall

Curator of Education:
Erin Branham

Curatorial Assistant:
Leslie Garrett

Curatorial Assistant:
Anne Gochenour

Preparator:
Keith Melton

ISBN 1-884240-27-5

Printer:
Davco Graphics

Photo Credits:
Camera Works

except:
Jane Sauer p. 89 photo credit Wendy McEahem

Editor:
Thom Hall

In all dimensions height precedes width precedes depth.

Introduction

Baskets Now: USA—a celebration of contemporary baskets by established and emerging artists working with traditional and exotic materials, fabrication methods, and forms—evolved and was ultimately shaped by a series of events interwoven much like the fibers of one of the baskets in the exhibition. Over a sixteen year period the Arkansas Arts Center began to exhibit and collect contemporary baskets; increasing interest in contemporary objects led to the renovation of the Pike-Fletcher-Terry House as the home of the Arkansas Arts Center Decorative Arts Museum; the museum received the gift of a significant body of contemporary baskets from the Diane and Sandy Besser Collection; and the new National Basketry Organization (NBO) emerged.

The collection's first contemporary baskets were knotted nylon fabrications by Memphis artist Patti Lechmann purchased from the museum's 15th and 16th Prints, Drawings, and Crafts competitions in 1982 and 1983. Next came Dona Look's *Birch Basket #2611* purchased from the first craft biennial *National Craft Invitational* in 1987 followed by Lillian Elliott's *Wheat* and John Garrett's *Beaded Pod Basket* purchased in 1989 from the second, more aptly named, *National Objects Invitational*. Museum director and chief curator Townsend Wolfe organized both of these exhibitions.

During this time Diane and Sandy Besser, residents of Little Rock and Santa Fe, New Mexico, were privately amassing an impressive collection of contemporary baskets in addition to their contemporary ceramic teapots, contemporary British ceramics, and works on paper. Their interest in baskets evolved with a visit to the *American Craft Today: Poetry of the Physical* exhibition at the American Craft Museum in New York (October 1986-March 1987). There they saw the work of Ed Rossbach, John McQueen, and others. On an American Craft Museum tour of Mildred Constantine's apartment they discovered the work of Kay Sekimachi and ultimately purchased a Sekimachi as their first basket. At Constantine's they also met textile designer and collector Jack Lenor Larsen who subsequently steered them to other basketmakers. By the late 1980s, a time when very little literature was available on the subject, the Bessers had nearly one hundred baskets in their collection.

In the mid-1990s, after nearly a decade of collecting baskets, the couple escalated their pattern of donating works of art to the museum's collections by giving a major portion of the contemporary baskets from the Diane and Sandy Besser Collection to the Arkansas Arts Center. Overnight the museum's collection swelled to seventy-eight baskets, and the museum was established as having one of the premier collections of contemporary baskets in the United States. For museum visitors, this impressive body of works opened a unique window to the world of contemporary basketry from the mid-1880s to the early 1990s while the museum gained access to basket artisans, dealers, and collectors—all at a time when the field was undergoing rapid change.

Later, in the summer of 1999, the museum lent some of its baskets to an exhibition and mini-basket conference organized by Michael Davis and Martha Connell through the auspices of the Handweavers Guild of America, Inc. This history-making conference, *Tradition & Innovation: Basketry Today*, was held at the Arrowmont School of Arts and Crafts in Gatlinburg, Tennessee. Through open discussions among the participants at the conference, there arose the need for an organization with basketry as its exclusive mission. A year later the National Basketry Organization was formed, and the Arkansas Arts Center offered to organize a major exhibition and to host the new organization for its first regional workshop.

The premise for *Baskets Now: USA* is to showcase established and emerging American basketmakers. For structure, an ad hoc exhibition committee was formed consisting of Lissa Hunter, Jane Sauer, Michel Davis, John Skau, Carole Eckert, and John Garrett. Each was asked to submit a list, ranked in groups of ten, of fifty of the most influential basketmakers working today. From the compilation of lists, the Arkansas Arts Center put together a roster and invited twenty-five artists to send two works each. Juror Jack Lenor Larsen selected an additional twenty-seven artists from a competition that was announced through letters, press releases, and the National Basketry Organization newsletter.

The museum wishes to express its appreciation to all who worked on the project with special thanks to Michael Davis and Helene Meyers who helped coordinate activities between the museum and the NBO. We also would like to thank Brad Cushman, director of the UALR art galleries, for organizing a companion exhibition of contemporary Japanese bamboo basketry from the Tia/Textile Arts Gallery of Santa Fe, and to John McGuire for organizing for the NBO the *Tradition Bearers* exhibition in the museum's lower lobby and lecture hall gallery. We are grateful to Robyn and John Horn for their support and for their sponsorship of the exhibition and catalogue and the opening activities.

Baskets today are not always containers as they were in the past. This exhibition includes both traditional baskets, containers made by interlacing natural fibers such as grass, reeds, bark, and pine needles available to hunters and gatherers of the past, and those more concerned with artistic expression. An art basket, now more commonly referred to as a "new basket," is a three-dimensional contemporary object with a structure consisting of interlaced short flexible fibers or slats. The basketmaker interested in the new basket is typically open to innovative ideas and diverse materials and techniques. The more traditional basketmaker of today tends to refine styles, techniques, and materials of the past. Their forms are pure and appeal to the modern eye.

Whether the "new basket" or the "traditional basket," today's basket is, first of all, an object made for contemplation. It serves more of an aesthetic purpose than a utilitarian one. It is intended to delight the eye and be admired for its satisfying form, its relationship to traditional basketmaking around the world, to our environment, to the art of our times, and for the artist's innovative ideas and sheer bravado, and for its intellectual and spiritual content. Today's baskets stretch our understanding of what we know; they preserve and honor the traditions of the past while exploring the new ideas and materials and techniques of the future.

Alan Du Bois

Artists

In this catalogue, names designated by a " ♦ " symbol denotes invited artists; others are artists juried by Jack Lenor Larsen. Illustrated work is indicated by a " ■ " symbol.

Jackie Abrams

(b. 1949, New York, NY; lives in Brattleboro, VT)

My work is about the possibilities of basketry—the possibilities of materials, of techniques, of colors and textures. It is a constant learning process, a progression of explorations. I am intrigued by the combinations of materials and techniques, the layers in a basket, and the painted surfaces that look like stone or leather or ceramics. I am strongly inspired by architecture, other cultures, and the world around me. The challenge to keep exploring satisfies my sense of creative wonder.

My roots in basketry are strongly grounded in tradition. In 1975 I apprenticed to Ben Higgins, an eighty-one-year-old basketmaker who worked with white ash. For 13 years I wove traditional, functional baskets of natural materials. In 1984 I started to further explore the aesthetic possibilities of basketry. I've been working with archival cotton paper, an extremely versatile and user-friendly material, since 1990.

My current choice of colors is strongly influenced by my trips to Australia; in October I returned from a teaching journey to Tasmania, Melbourne and Sydney. I expect the ochres and reds to continue to have a strong influence in my work.

This year I received a creation grant from the Vermont Arts Council—to construct a series of architectural structures using fiber techniques. I explored the possibilities of combining paper with copper sheeting and black ash strips, of creating urban skyscrapers that interact with each other. I am intrigued by the negative spaces (the windows) that encourage further exploration on the part of the viewer. I am excited to see where this takes me.

■ The Springtime of Her Life, 2001
archival cotton paper, acrylic paint, varnish, copper wire
14 x 8 x 6 inches

Darryl and Karen Arawjo

(b. 1953, Allentown & Bethlehem, PA; live in Bushkill, PA)

We have been full time basketmakers for the past twenty years. In that time we have worked mainly with traditional materials and techniques and also designed many original styles. The idea for the LightVessels came to Darryl one day as he watched his fishing line glistening on the water. Struck by the play of light, he decided to try to capture that magic in a basket. The foundation of the baskets remains firmly in tradition as we use handsplit oak or hickory for the framework. The weaving is monofilament that gives the LightVessel its translucent, glowing aura. The bottoms and rims, hand-turned on a lathe, provide contrast and grace to the finished basket. We enjoy the classic form of these baskets; they have graceful curves and clean lines.

We continue to experiment and explore the infinite possibilities that this new technique has opened for us.

■ Light Vessel CXC, 2001
white oak, hickory, monofilament, walnut
9 1/2 x 8 1/2 inches diameter

'Dorothy Gill Barnes

(b. 1927, Strawberry Point, IO; lives in Worthington, OH)

My intent is to construct a vessel or related object using materials respectfully harvested from nature. Nature's variety—including fine fern stems and heavy chunks of wood, bark or stone—provides a rich cache of supplies, often almost overpowering in stimulation and opportunity for design. My processes include traditional weaving techniques and experimentation. Small needles and power tools in the studio enable me to create 2-inch miniatures and pieces 10 feet long. Some works could be made in half an hour, and others planned, grown, cut and constructed over a period of years. The result may be an ephemeral or an archival work. The unique properties I find in gathered materials suggest a process for each piece.

My work in this medium started in the early 1970s, encouraged by Ruth Mary Papenthien, Jack Lenor Larson, my husband Marshall, and those who offered wonderful gathering opportunities. I was excited by the work of Ed Rossbach and later John McQueen, who set a standard for many using materials from nature.

I hope that my structures, some of which are basketlike, honor the growing things from which they came.

■ Above and Below the Earth, 1999
mulberry wood, bark, roots
11 x 14 x 13 inches
From the Collection of Ed & Jo Pascoe

Two Baskets from a Pine Branch, 2001
white pine
6 1/2 x 20 x 8 inches

•Nancy Moore Bess

(b. 1943, Arbuckle, CA; lives in Amherst, MA)

I have always had a bias toward symbols, nuances, and subtleties. So, not unexpectedly, the extended periods of time I spent in Japan were, and continue to be, a significant influence on the way I see life, the way I appreciate daily artifacts, and the way I relate to objects. I have developed a new attitude toward and liking for certain, simple materials—rice straw used to enclose, protect and enhance multiples, folded paper to present a gift, and a single piece of bamboo, cut and bent into elaborate curves for a *sake* bottle used in New Year's rituals. I choose reminders of interesting lines, silhouettes and forms—e.g. temple bells, newel posts, and the layering within woven fences and armor.

Many of my vessel forms are permanently closed to suggest treasures, secrets, and ritual. While I twine, I often refer back to the place or object that was the inspiration/model for the work in progress. In remembering, I work to infuse the vessel with the sensations and imagery evoked.

■ "JAKAGO" (snake basket) III, 2001
waxed cord, Japanese bamboo
5 1/2 x 8 x 5 1/2 inches

Tea Jar, 2001
waxed cord, Japanese bamboo, Japanese ornament
5 x 3 1/4 inches diameter

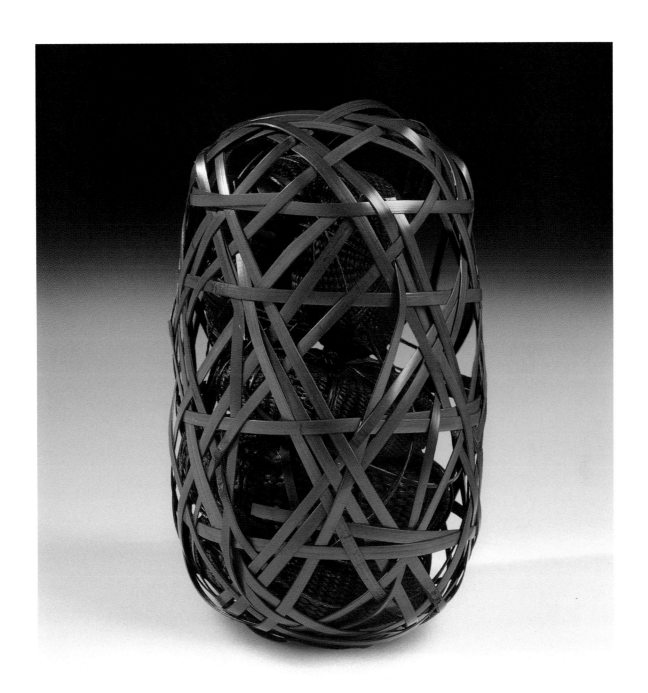

˙Jerry Bleem

(b. 1954, Red Bud, IL; lives in Cicero, IL)

I am fascinated by the human need to create meaning and to order reality. Taking the disparate elements of life and making sense of them has always been the cultural task. This construction of truth delineates a system from which we can orientate ourselves. Though the ability to find some "absolute" is implied, the process is quite arbitrary.

The forms I make are likewise the result of ordering individual elements in a constructive process. Each singular result denies innumerable other possibilities. However, intention is not the entire story; a coincidence of accidents also helps to create these pieces. Though I begin with a clear idea, the unfolding of the work invariably changes my initial concept. It is in the course of putting these sculptures together that their forms actually emerge.

All of my pieces have openings. At times these allow the interiors of the works to be readily seen. In other instances, the inside can only be seen through the viewers' imagination. In part, these entries are thresholds where inside meets outside, where "heaven meets earth"—in the language of Mircea Eliade. I think of these openings as orifices of access, as places of passage.

Ordinary, non-precious, discarded, found materials are what I most often use in my work. (My life is more frequently informed by the ordinary than by what is extraordinary or exceptional.) I do not employ any armatures or any adhesives besides staples. The torque from each applied piece both creates the form and gives it strength.

Botanic forms and the human body have strongly influenced my work. I also draw upon humanity's long history of constructing containers for both practical and symbolic purposes. These hollow forms imply both a presence now absent, and a potential not yet present.

I make work to contemplate life and the mystery inherent in living.

June 10, 1983, 2000
found metal printing plate, staples
12 1/4 x 19 1/4 x 11 1/2 inches

■ Analogy, 2001
found plastic, thread, staples
19 x 19 x 15 inches

Joan Brink

(b. 1945, New Orleans, LA; lives in Santa Fe, NM)

In terms of placing myself within the craft and tradition of basketry, I occupy that corner dedicated to the Lightship baskets originating on Nantucket Island, MA. It is with this form and method that I have concerned myself over the past decade. Very important in my development as a basket weaver has been my on-going inspiration by American Indian baskets.

In the 1970s I began weaving coiled baskets influenced by Marvin Cohodas, a skilled weaver and an authority on the baskets of Dat so la lee. A master weaver and designer from the Washoe tribe early in the twentieth century, her work touched my creative spirit above all others, inspiring me to reach toward the perfection of the craft in the context of my own artistic vision.

Coming from a basketry tradition (Nantucket) known generally more for style and function than content, it is no wonder that I found the design and color of American Indian basketry inspirational. For me the creation of a simple 'language' of symbols led to a fascination with the basket as a rich vehicle for narrative content. The idea or 'story' for each vessel is expressed through select colorful symbols: the evolving object becomes imbued with the idea during the month-long meditation of weaving.

The shapes of the baskets have become full and embody curves born out of the application of sacred geometry. I feel the baskets succeed when there is harmonious balance between shape, materials, design and symbolic content. When this happens the woven vessels are empowered with the beauty to which I aspire and which I found early on in the masterpieces of Dat so la lee. Although my baskets embrace tradition, they also step quietly beyond.

■ Peace Prayer, 2001
cane, dyed and bleached, satinwood rim & base
10 1/2 x 18 inches diameter

Deb Curtis

(b. 1956, Freeport, TX; lives in Corvallis, OR)

Baskets are a tradition that is changing. I explore both traditional and contemporary forms of basketry. Many of my baskets blend both forms to create "new" baskets. My traditional work uses authentic materials and methods. My contemporary work often combines mediums. Recent works link traditional basket weaving with tapestry weaving, beading, stitching, and surface design. Designs for the baskets come from objects found in the natural world or from a feeling that I have while creating the basket. By blending colors and textures I change the character of the basket from a functional vessel only, to a container that expresses a concept. Renewable native North American materials are utilized and I personally gather all of my Pacific Northwest materials. I strive to show that there is beauty in tradition and purpose to contemporary basketry.

■ The Past Surrounds the Present, 2001
birch bark, cedar bark, northwest sweetgrass
13 x 5 1/2 x 1 1/2 inches

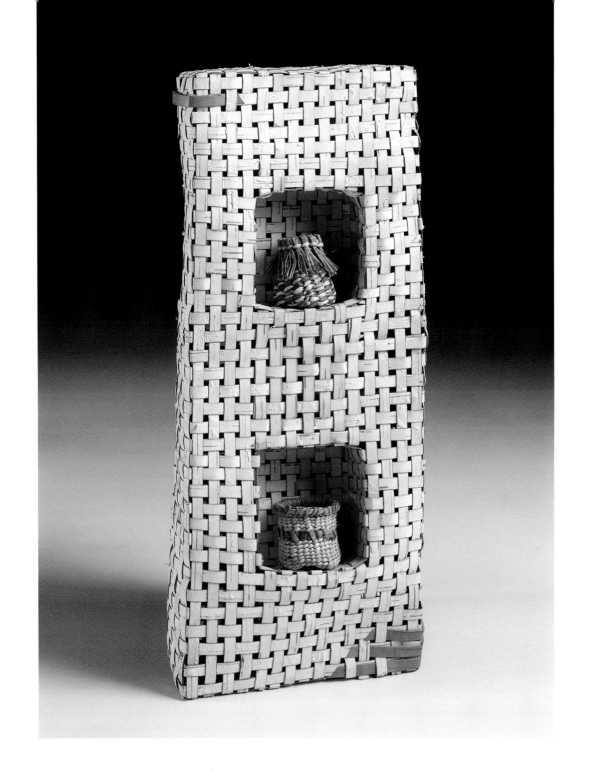

◆Michael Davis

(b. 1952, Jacksonville, FL; lives in Roswell, GA)

My tightly woven forms are classical and sculptural and are directly influenced by my pottery and painting background. I love to manipulate bold and primary colors of enamel and acrylic paint onto the surfaces of my baskets.

In all my work, whether large or small, I use a sixty-four ribbed structure (armature), and rely on basic basket materials for structural as well as textural manipulations. Altering these unassuming materials by cutting, stitching, painting, and patterning, I strive to create complex yet conciliatory twined forms.

■ Medieval Pinecone 200, 2000
reed, acrylic, enamel paint
12 x 14 inches diameter

Celestial Series—Three Full Moons, 1998
reed, acrylic, enamel paint, ash, Styrofoam
35 x 23 x 20 inches

˙Carol Eckert

(b. 1945, Chapel Hill, NC; lives in Tempe, AZ)

I use an ancient basketry technique, coiling, to construct contemporary allegorical vessels and staffs. All of the forms are coiled with cotton thread over a wire core, using the figure-eight stitch. My pieces sometimes tell a story and I often use a recurring "cast of characters" to refer to certain mythological themes. My recent baskets are becoming more complex and slightly larger as I continue to explore the universal nature of animal symbols in legends, myths, and spiritual traditions.

■ Tale of Three Ravens, 2001
cotton, wire
12 1/2 x 16 x 3 1/2 inches

Processional Iguanas, 2001
cotton, wire, wood
72 x 13 x 4 inches

Kathey Ervin

(b. 1952, Raymond, WA; lives in Sequim, WA)

I am an artist/basket maker who has crafted containers from nature's resources for thirty years. Gathering materials is an inspiration in itself, as I study the shapes and reflected patterns of nature. There is complexity and rhythm and a sense of discovery in the woods that I strive to bring into my baskets.

■ Button Basket, 2000
western red cedar bark (natural and dyed),
Alaskan yellow bark, antique mother of pearl buttons
15 x 11 x 4 inches

Jacquie R. Fort

(b. 1949, Ithaca, NY; lives in Vero Beach, FL)

Having been a fiber artist for over twenty years, I find myself gravitating towards indigenous organic material incorporating found objects and collage material. The results produce a fiber work where the image and the medium are responded to. The use of unconventional weaving materials encourages me to take into account other options and directions that are not readily apparent: "forcing my hand," one could say. I find myself discovering many perimeters of basketry by exploring the nature of these materials and all their many intangibles. As a result, it is a very freeing and cathartic method where nothing is privileged which results in a variety of surface designs and woven reed forms of infinite variety. The vein of continuity running through most of my basketry observes a sense of antiquity, ancient times, and ritual artifacts of unpremeditated origin with a strong sense of energy.

■ Journey of a Thousand Miles, 2001
fiber, collage, canvas, datu rattan,
natural vine, palm coir, waxed linen
32 x 16 x 7 inches

⁺John Garrett

(b. 1950, El Paso, TX; lives in Albuquerque, NM)

Why baskets? I use the basket form and the idea of baskets (that is, a handmade vessel of interconnected available materials) because they allow me to do so many things with a myriad of materials. Since baskets have served so many purposes: utilitarian, decorative, and ceremonial, I can make forms that relate to traditional works. Maybe my basket will tell a story or make a statement or ask a question. I like building with unusual materials not usually associated with basketry. I collect and salvage materials from the street, the desert, yard sales, and flea markets. Informal pieces may lead me to a series of works that become increasingly refined. Likewise, a formal piece may suggest some new expressive ways I might use my materials. There are always connections involved in building baskets. The physical connections act as an excellent metaphor for the meanings of my work.

■ Baroque Boat Basket No. 3, 2001
aluminum, paint, hardware cloth, wire
14 x 24 x 16 inches

Untitled, 2001
copper, steel, hardware cloth, wire, beads
24 x 18 x 18 inches

*Mary Giles

(b. 1944, St. Paul, MN; lives in St. Louis, MO)

My baskets, although non-functional, sculptural works, are connected to the utilitarian pieces of my predecessors. I am indebted to the multitude of makers from many cultures, from today and ancient times.

The colors and surfaces in nature, particularly as they accumulate age and reflect light, are major sources of inspiration.

In my years of working I have learned that a finished piece is not an end but the beginning of the next piece. All the new is in the past.

■ Shadows of Freedom, 1990
waxed linen, wire
18 x 5 inches diameter
Private Collection

Totem with Shadow, 1999
waxed linen, iron, copper
22 x 6 x 2 1/2 inches (totem)
50 1/2 x 6 1/4 inches (shadow)
Private Collection

Patti Hawkins

(b. 1950, Tallahassee, FL; lives in Moline, IL)

I believe that people seem to fall into two distinctly different categories—those who happily go through life with an organized routine and predictable days—and those who embrace the unpredictable, driven by a passion for creative expression. I am definitely in the latter category! As a child, my mother taught me almost every form of needlework, and my musician father inspired me to become an accomplished pianist. My discovery of basketmaking seventeen years ago seemed to be a natural progression from my up-bringing. I was accustomed to working with my hands, and found that musical rhythms logically translate into the rhythms of weaving, especially twills.

I first discovered basketry when pregnant with my fourth child, and found it to be the perfect outlet for my creativity while allowing me to be at home with my family. I have taught extensively for years, finding my psychology background invaluable for successful individualized instruction. As much as I have loved teaching, in the past few years I have focused more on creating exhibit baskets, purely for the love of self-expression. Now that my children are becoming young adults, I am excited about having more time for my work—and I can't wait to see where it takes me!

I have experimented with almost every form of basketry, but am primarily drawn to the mathematical symmetry and natural rhythms of twill weaves. Incorporating a variety of textures and layers is also a focus of my current work, which has been inspired by the handwork I learned as a child. It never ceases to amaze me how all the joy and pain in life combine to influence my basketry, and how infinite the possibilities are!

■ Covering, 2001
dyed and natural rattan, waxed linen
9 1/2 x 8 inches diameter

Jan Henry

(b. 1948, Austell, GA; lives in Lithonia, GA)

When I began my basketmaking career, I used dyes and was even known to use curls now and then. Times have changed and my work is at once more simple and more complicated. I gather my white oak and other woods from nature and shape them into baskets with more character and less glitter. An architectural overlay has begun to emerge and I am more concerned with textures, layers, and wood joinery. This basket is the seventh in a series that explores the sunburst design, but it is the first to incorporate only woods from our property. I'm having such fun!

■ Ode to Stickley, 2001
hand-split white oak, quarter-sawn
white oak, hand-braided leather
8 x 11 x 6 inches
Private Collection

⁕Pat Hickman

(b. 1941, Ft. Morgan, CO; lives in Honolulu, HI)

Layering and surface, humble and sophisticated, familiar and unfamiliar, simple and complex—all add to the richness and potential meaning in Art. I wonder about paired opposites. Playing with them allows me to explore a broad range of expression, all related to shared human experience. Ideas of skin, both plant and and animal skin and membranes and verbal expressions about skin interest me—"skin deep," "under one's skin," "thick skinned," "chicken skin," and many more. These all seem close to life, suggesting depth to me, something beneath a thin (skin) surface.

I want to see where I can go when I enter the uncertain place of art making, into an unknown arena, outside of usual borders, wherever that takes me. It's about seeing more, seeing differently, and continually learning to see. It's serious play.

Chew Out, 1998
gut (hog casings), indigo dye
7 x 8 1/2 x 12 inches

■ North, 2000
birch, gut (hog casings), waxed linen, acrylic,
colored ink, metallic stick, indigo dye
19 x 9 x 6 inches

Patti Quinn Hill

(b. 1948, New Orleans, LA; lives in Weaverville, NC)

Wild Fire!!!

As I weave these pieces, I am inspired by the three fires that engulf these, my Smokey Mountains. This is not the blue mist smoke that is usually seen in these beautiful, pristine, breath-taking vistas. We have not had rain in two months, so the fires blaze on, and on, and on. As I weave and gaze out my window, I wait for rain…

My work rests on traditional structure, but has it's own spirit and grace. "Fire on the Mountains" is a contemporary spin-off from Shaker influence. Shaker baskets are totally traditional and very technical. So working in the medium of paper allows me to have fun with all of this technique, structure, and detail that can sometimes be confining, and it makes for a good marriage with creativity and originality. I use a number of kinds of surface design techniques to get the color on the paper. My baskets have a continuous flow, and the feet give them a light perky feeling. The curls add texture and an added dimension, which I find interesting and intriguing. As you walk around a piece, the "eyes" if you will, follow you. There is a lightness, movement, and activity happening from a totally still object.

My greatest pleasure in the process is to sit back and view my finished work, and I enjoy the thought of sharing a part of myself with the world that will endure long after I am gone.

■ Fire on the Mountains, 2001
100% cotton archival paper, paint, metallic thread
8 1/2 x 9 1/2 inches diameter
5 1/2 x 9 1/2 x 6 3/4 inches
15 1/2 x 6 1/2 inches diameter

Jan Hopkins

(b. 1955, Nampa, ID; lives in Everett, WA)

My emphasis has been contemporary basketry with natural materials. The majority of my training has been with traditional basket makers. The lessons I have learned from traditional masters are not only the technique, but also the process; knowing when to gather, how to prepare, and which materials I can use with the various techniques. This knowledge has increased my ability to work with and explore alternative materials.

This piece, entitled "The Grass is Always Greener…" was inspired by the work of M.C. Escher and traditional basketry. The mathematics and repetition of pattern is very much like the process found in traditional basketry. Though my techniques and materials are not traditional, the process leads me back to my traditional training.

■ The Grass is Always Greener, 2001
grapefruit peel, waxed linen, hemp paper
14 x 16 x 6 inches

'Lissa Hunter

(b. 1945, Indianapolis, IN; lives in Portland, ME)

It all goes back to my childhood, growing up in Indiana. My father was a salesman and a magician; my mother, a secretary and an untrained artist. Through their immense love for us, they saw my brother and me as distinct individuals, the authors of our own lives.

There weren't so many things in the world then, but it seemed that most of them were in our home. A Victorian organ no one knew how to play, a Chinese opium pipe brought back by missionary ancestors, a garden fountain in the kitchen because Mom liked the sound of water, antique cars in the garage, a small Tibetan cabinet with many drawers, a human skull Dad had won in a poker game when he was twenty-one, all kept company with many more seemingly unrelated objects.

They all had histories. I loved knowing that many of them had belonged to other people whose lives were so different from my own. I could only imagine their stories and add my own experiences to create new tales that were as real to me as the things themselves.

Someone was always sewing, tinkering with an engine, painting woodwork, fixing a bicycle, braiding a rug, taking something apart or putting something together in our home. We were a family of makers, by necessity and temperament. The process of making was how we interacted with life and each other.

I am still making objects, intrigued by structures and materials, creating histories even I don't know. The stories come later, when a viewer adds his or her own experiences to these objects, creating another history and new tales.

Fog, 2001
wood, paper, drywall compound,
paint, pencils, wire, waxed linen
16 x 40 x 3 inches

■ Ten Bowls, 2000
wood, paper, drywall compound,
paint, pencil, wire, waxed linen
24 x 16 x 3 inches

♦Kiyomi Iwata

(b. 1941, Kobe, Japan; lives in Valley Cottage, NY)

The Japanese tradition of *furoshiki* which is a square cloth tied at the center, *furoshiki*, for the purpose of carrying objects inspired me to make the "Fold" series. The intrigue of wrapping an unknown content or mystery, fabricated by two opposite materials, silk and metal, as one can see in eighteenth century Japanese armor, continues to stimulate energy in me.

■ Bronze Fold #5, 1997
brass woven cloth, gold leaves, French
embroidery knots, painted silk organza
7 x 7 1/2 x 5 inches

Bronze Fold #8, 1999
brass woven cloth, aluminum mesh,
gold leaves, stuffed silk gold leaf tubes
5 1/2 x 7 x 4 1/2 inches

*Mary Jackson

(b. 1945, Mount Pleasant, SC; lives in Charleston, SC)

It was always so amazing to me to see my mother make incredibly beautiful baskets from materials gathered from the wild. Learning all of the basic techniques and traditional designs from her took years of practice and determination. When I had mastered the traditional forms, I became bored. I felt that I had to do something new. I wanted to make my own special contribution to the art, so I started designing contemporary forms that had never been done in this tradition before.

The transformation of age-old shapes has emerged into a more challenging dimension, and I am now celebrating a new and calm body of work. The technique is the same; the material is the same as in the traditional baskets; it's just stretching the tradition to the limit of an art form.

I've always believed that whatever's worth doing is worth doing well. My goal is constantly to produce simple, yet unique and finely detailed sculpture in which the patterns and symmetry complement each other.

Strong feelings and deep emotions are involved in making my baskets, so it is always exciting to make a new idea reality. Particular attention to form and function is of utmost importance, because my tradition has always emphasized a beautiful basket to be used for everyday living. It is my commitment to my ancestors to work within this context.

■ Accordion, 2000
sweetgrass, bulrush, palmetto
16 1/2 x 10 x 9 inches

Traditional Market Basket, 2001
sweetgrass, pine needles, bulrush, palmetto
12 x 15 x 19 inches

*Ferne Jacobs

(b. 1942, Chicago, IL; lives in Los Angeles, CA)

My work has gone from painting to weaving, and then in 1970, I began to create three-dimensional fiberwork using ancient basketmaking techniques, which I remain committed to today. This commitment grows out of a fascination that thread can be made solid, that by using only my hands and the thread, a form can be made that will physically stand on its own.

Doing work of this kind makes me feel a deep connection to a timeless past that emerges out of the earth. I am a link in bringing this ancient way of being into my own time, hopefully making it relevant as an art form, and helping nurture it into the future.

I see this piece in my mind that is never finished. It is constantly in motion and changing and yet is one and the same. To stay with the form each time until it becomes itself is my goal, knowing that this is the current moment and then the shift will occur again. The excitement for me is in the details, going so slow that I spend a great amount of time in them. It is as if I can find the form through the details, creating a body that emerges by each wrap of the thread, cell by cell.

At the end of a film I saw, "Ulysses' Gaze" was its name, a character playing a filmmaker says the following: "I will return with a new name. I will tell you about the lemon tree outside your home and about the moon. In between embraces I will tell you a story, the story that never ends, the unending story."

To me, this is what all art is about, how the flow of making it feels continuous, as does the process of seeing it.

■ Centric Spaces, 2000
coiled and twined waxed linen thread
15 x 12 x 11 inches

Open Globe, 2001
coiled and twined waxed linen thread
13 x 13 inches diameter

Donna Kallner

(1958, Kokomo, IN; lives in White Lake, WI)

From my current vantage point, which is past the midpoint of the biblical age of three score and ten, I see patterns in life that I couldn't appreciate when I was younger. When I stitch a piece like this, I think about how each moment is connected to what came before and what is yet to come, and I marvel at how side trips that seem to go nowhere add richness to the journey.

■ Three Score and Ten, 2001
coiled Siberian iris leaves stitched with Irish linen
8 3/4 x 7 1/2 x 5 1/2 inches

Donna Kaplan

(b. 1942, New Jersey; lives in North Bend, WA)

I live at the base of a steeply ascending 4,416-foot mountain. The mountain changes color and mood constantly. Living in this environment greatly influences my perception, mood and use of color. I cannot ignore my environment. Thus much of my work concerns the environment and our human imprint upon the world. In addition, having spent many years working as a clinical nurse specialist and occupational therapist in the field of psychiatry, I find that I cannot ignore our collective and individual human psyche. All of these influences find their way into my work. I attempt to convey memories and shadows of memories. My work conveys fragments of stories from my experiences and from those around me.

I use metal, fiber, glass, beads, and paint as materials and fiber techniques to provide structure. My work is woven on a loom utilizing a wire warp or spranged on a frame. The metal is sewn and manipulated into shape using pliers and my hands. Occasionally I embellish my work with embroidery. I have found woven metal and sprang a satisfying way to convey my ideas in three-dimensional form.

About *Undulations*

This work came about after living through a 6.8 earthquake. The earth moved and rolled, the trees were waving and crashing to the ground around me and landslides were falling down our mountain in great clouds of dust and rock and debris. Undulations is a reflection of that experience.

▪ Undulations, 2001
loom woven metal with linen,
silk and metallic threads
24 x 16 inches diameter
Private Collection

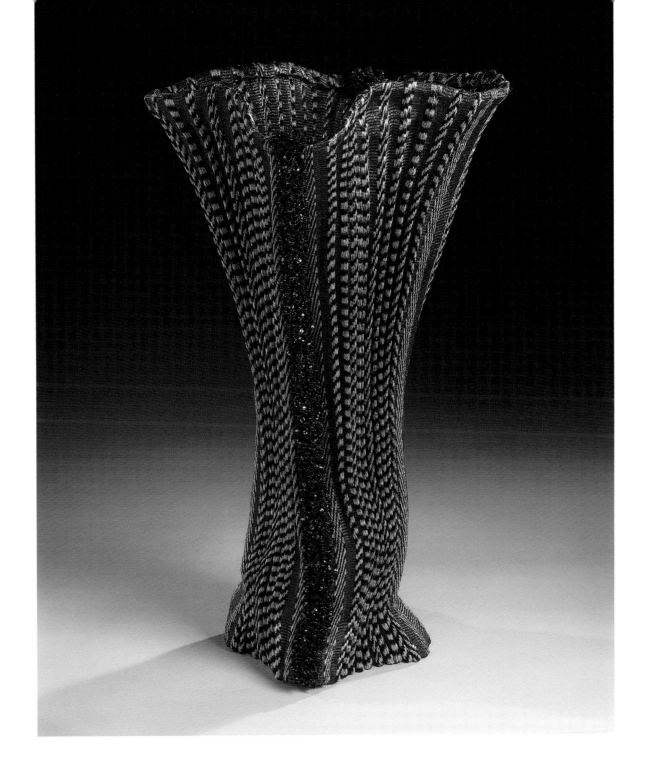

Susan kavichy

(b. 1953, Berwyn, IL; lives in Island Lake, IL)

The focus of my work is process oriented.

Several years ago, I was significantly changed by the process of finding a brown ash tree, harvesting it from the swamp, removing its bark, pounding its growth rings, removing and splitting the splints, sizing the splints, and weaving a basket with those very splints. Revealed by the arduous pounding of the tree and tedious splitting of the splints, is a lush, satiny surface with remarkable, inherent surface variations. This fiber is extremely durable and versatile and has an unassuming quality of strength. Though I no longer process the material myself, I am no less inspired. My delight is to continually explore the qualities of brown ash.

Weaving the brown ash keeps me centered. Because of its satiny surface, I must stay centered. When my mind drifts, the ash can easily twist, and I am pulled to the present by the necessity to unweave and weave again. In this way, brown ash becomes teacher, and my lesson is to listen to what the energy of the creative process is saying: "Surrender beyond the mundane. Accept the development of the piece in the moment." Pushing my capacity for tolerating the discomfort of not knowing the outcome and staying put while surrendering to the void is necessary for authentic work to come forth. A willingness to learn the pace of the piece is unrelenting. The mystery unfolding is simultaneously, unnerving and thrilling. As I maintain this student relationship to the piece, a true communion occurs, and it is through that communion that the tree is transformed.

■ Scepter and Bell, 2000
brown ash and yarn
13 x 13 x 15 1/2 inches

˙Gyöngy Laky

(b. 1944, Budapest, Hungary; lives in San Francisco, CA)

A stone's throw from the next century, artists are stitching with thorns, carving logs, braiding hillsides, drawing with sticks, writing poems on leaves, and growing sculpture. I am drawn to this type of work and feel I am a participant in this quiet, but significant art movement. The outdoors has long been a source of inspiration to artists, but the present explorations suggest a new relationship, entreat a lighter hand, acknowledge a greater interdependence, and propose a more profound respect.

Much of my sculpture, site-specific outdoor work, and basketry over the past several years, reference my concern for environmental issues. They are primarily composed of orchard debris, park trimmings, and street tree prunings. I collect from the many tons of cuttings which are available each year as growers and gardeners trim and discard (or often burn) the branches of nut and fruit trees and as we maintain our parks, streets and gardens. I am interested in making a small dent in changing attitudes about the environment and our relationship to it. I play with the question of "what is waste?" when I work elements from nature which have been discarded by humans.

Simple procedures and the directness of hand-built construction appeal to me. My work draws upon basic forms of human ingenuity about building things. Fascination with simple, improvisational constructions such as scaffolding and fences has led me to experiment with structures and materials emphasizing linear arrangements in what I consider working in the architectural spectrum. This approach provides an ingenious array of ways to form materials into vessels, sculptures and wall pieces.

■ Amphibios II, 2001
mandarin prunings, sheet rock bullets
9 1/2 x 16 inches diameter

Possible Comfort, 2001
toothpicks, brown eggs
6 x 16 inches diameter

⬧Patti Lechmann

(b. 1946, Fort Bragg, NC; lives in Memphis, TN)

The vessel, the archetypal female form has been central to my work for more than 25 years, whether the vessels were made of clay or fiber. Both materials are associated with Neolithic civilizations that produced vessels in clay and fiber to store and carry grain, water, wine…life giving substances.

The pieces represent a life spirit for me, which is why mythologies, Hindu, Buddhist, Greek, and Egyptian figure so strongly in my titles. Creation myths, stories of birth, death, beauty, evil, fire, sun and moon, sky and seasons, ideas central to all life seem to me a vital way to connect with who we are, where we come from, what we all share—our commonalities as humans.

I want to work to celebrate those ideas since I feel our ability to celebrate has been so damaged by contemporary angst, fear, mistrust, and cynicism. Our spirit of joy and beauty must live in spite of the pain of existence. I make no apologies for wanting my work to delight visually. I hope it has grace and elegance, that it can make the spirit soar, maybe briefly, but joyfully, as a celebration of life and the resilience of the Human spirit.

Nicchū (Day), 2001
knotted nylon with glass beads
5 1/2 x 5 1/2 x 1 1/4 inches

■ Nikkō (Sunrise), 2001
knotted nylon with glass beads
6 x 4 1/4 x 2 1/2 inches

⁺Kari Lønning

(b. 1950, Torrington, CT; lives in Ridgefield, CT)

All my life I knew that I would make and build things. I began college as a jewelry and metalsmithing major, but I graduated as a potter. Along the way, I studied design and became interested in weaving. But nothing clicked. Jewelry was too "tight," ceramics required too much equipment, and I was always wet and dirty, and my weaving couldn't physically stand up by itself. When I began weaving rattan baskets, everything fell into place. I could weave thrown forms and build complex constructions.

Although rattan continues to offer me countless challenges, I became intrigued with a new material. Every winter I saved orange crates for some future use. The printed graphics and clean plywood motivated me to cut them up and reassemble them into conical forms. At first, I just tied the pieces together with waxed linen. Then I glued in bases to give them strength and to maintain their shapes. As I got more involved with these vessel forms, I found myself building double-walled constructions reminiscent of the ones I wove in rattan. In addition to the patterned orange crates, now I also buy and use commercial plywoods. The lure of recycling the crates and creating classic forms has sparked my imagination. Some day, I may paint these pieces, build them larger or construct them in metal with cables. The possibilities are endless.

Executive Tweed, 2001
Procion dyed and natural rattan reed, marbles
9 1/2 x 14 inches diameter

■ Tribute to the Connecticut
Commission on the Arts #3, 2001
birch plywood, waxed linen thread
9 1/2 x 8 1/2 inches diameter

˙Dona Look

(b. 1948 Mequon, WI; lives in Algoma, WI)

Although I have had informal training in various fiber arts throughout my life and received a B.A. in art from the University of Wisconsin-Oshkosh in 1970, I am a self-taught basket maker.

I choose to work with white birch bark because of the unique qualities that make it suitable for both weaving and sewing. Although I continue to collect and experiment with other materials such as cedar, basswood bark, and willow, I prefer to concentrate on white birch bark. Because the quality of the bark is crucial to my work, I search out large, healthy trees that are soon to be logged. This process of gathering and preparing materials often dictates each tree's use. Technique and scale are determined by the length, thickness and elasticity of the bark. Subtle variations in proportion and color are dependent on the bark I have available. Since I begin my work in the forest, the resulting baskets may reflect my respect for these materials and my concern for the health and diversity of our northern woodlands.

Using techniques that I developed to create specific forms, I often work on a group of baskets together. Beginning with the preparation and cutting of bark for several pieces, but they are in fact parts of a continuous learning process.

Although I am interested in fiber arts from other cultures and times, my ideas are influenced by environment and come from memory and imagination. Innumerable fleeting images of forms seen in the past and hidden somewhere in the mind resurface by chance to be manipulated and altered by the imagination to fit the possibilities defined by the materials used. An idea may begin on the beach or in my garden, seeing the profile and volume of a pod or pumpkin. Using bark from the forest as fabric, the image is then altered to suit the materials.

I collect bark from trees that are being logged, since the stress and scars that result from peeling the bark will usually destroy the tree. There are subtle differences in the thickness and color of bark on each tree. Outer layers of bark are peeled away to provide a uniform surface. All pieces of bark are planned and cut before assembly. Side pieces are cut from the bark of one tree in order to match color and surface quality.

The top and bottom, as well as all the sides, are measured and sewn together with waxed silk thread. Edges along the side pieces are reinforced with narrow strips of bark. The top band is constructed of several layers of bark and sewn on with a hoop wrapped in waxed silk thread.

#982 Spiral, 1998
white birch bark, waxed silk thread
14 x 11 inches diameter

■ #969 Globe, 1996
white birch bark, waxed silk thread
13 1/2 x 12 1/2 inches diameter

·John McQueen

(b. 1943, Oakland, IL; resides in Saratoga Springs, NY)

I believe, in the beginning I wanted to make baskets because I found when I made a basket, the object I was making was the subject. If I asked what it was, the obvious answer was, it is a basket. This is different than any other art. If I am painting, I must paint something. Even if it is an abstraction, the painting is not what it is physically, but it is something else. It has subject matter attached to it. Sculpture is the same. It is a figure or abstract or something. What it is made from and the way it is made is not its reason for being. Baskets exist because they are baskets. The object is the subject.

In time, though, their most dominant characteristic, that they are containers, began to influence my thinking. I realized the term container is very broad and my basket opened up. This pushed the definition of traditional basket making, but to me almost everything is a container, and almost all physical objects have an inside and an outside. I began to look at objects that at first seemed either too large or long and narrow to be containers. This led me to lakes, rivers, what I thought of as "landscape containers." However, containers do not need to be physical objects. I explored ideas such as sentences having a beginning and an end and being contained within their beginning capital letter and their ending period. A concise thought is concise because it is contained. This more abstract thinking about baskets led me to, or maybe I should say back to, the physical aspects of the basket. Literally how it was put together. If the void or hole inside it makes it a basket, I wanted to place that void or space around each element. This would move the single large inside space to many, even thousands of very small spaces throughout the structure. The result was a solid object or an object that was structurally consistent all the way through, but full of many spaces.

■ Welcome, Welcome, 2001
willow branches, zip ties
104 x 27 inches diameter (each tower)

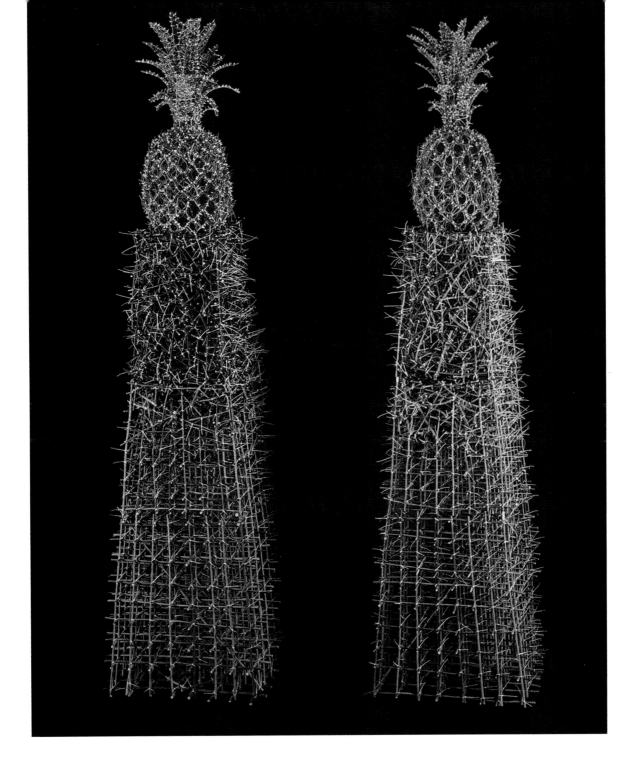

Mary Merkel-Hess

(b. 1949, Waterloo, IA; lives in Iowa City, IA)

I make baskets because I am fascinated by form and structure. I look for inspiration for form in the natural world, and then I allow technique to mesh with these visual ideas to create something new. I enjoy all aspects of this process: the appreciation of the world around me that suggests ideas and the search for a method of construction that lets my ideas take shape.

■ Two Hills, 2001
reed, paper
15 x 34 x 7 inches (each piece)

Sally Metcalf

(b. 1950, Burbank, CA; lives in Vida, OR)

The vessels that I make are woven of dyed and natural rattan reed. Fiber reactive dyes are used to color the reeds. I often incorporate stone, wood, and glass beads into the designs.

The first decision made in producing each vessel is the basic shape. Then I pick the colors, usually three to four that will enhance the shape. Even though the basic shape is in my mind, I rely on the process to guide my hands toward the final look. For instance, I might decide that by changing a certain weave the outcome of the piece would be better served. All my pieces are one of a kind and made by me alone.

The material is rattan reed, which is a wild and prolific vine from the rain forests of Southeast Asia. After the reed is harvested it is run through extruders to produce the various sizes and shapes. I then dye the material in my studio. The fiber reactive dyes used are color and light fast and produce a rich pallet of hues.

Inspiration for my work comes from my own backyard, the Cascade Mountains in western Oregon. The luscious greens and blues of the rain forest and the brilliant yellows, oranges, reds, and even the browns of the fall determine my pallet. The intense jungle-like quality of the forest as it grows and changes offers compelling weaving challenges.

■ Ember, 2001
dyed rattan reed, bone, glass beads
10 x 12 inches diameter

C.A. Michel

(b. 1951, Denver, CO; lives in Los Angeles, CA)

In these constructions feathers, individually beautiful but fragile, are assembled into strong vessels like elegant chariots soft yet secure, destined to carry a soul on its transmigration into the next world.

■ Wamba I, 2001
natural pheasant feathers,
wool and linen core
6 1/2 x 8 1/2 x 6 1/2 inches

*Norma Minkowitz

(b. 1937, New York, NY; lives in Westport, CT)

Containment means, to have within, to enclose, to confine, to be able to hold and restrict.

My sculptures enclose and confine, but they also expose. While the sculpture cannot be entered, the interior is visible through the exterior, which is a meshed cage. The element of light plays an important role in viewing my work. As the light changes, so does the dominance of the outer and inner forms. They exchange places.

At this time, my focus is to manipulate linear elements into personal and psychological statements, and both to enclose and expose a mysteriousness that invites contemplation.

■ Remembrance, 2001
paper pulp, wood, wire, resin, pencil
13 1/2 x 22 x 21 inches

The Wind Swallowed The Tree, 2001
paper pulp, wood, wire, pencil
13 1/2 x 28 x 9 inches

Benjia Morgenstern

(b. 1943, New York, NY; lives in North Bay Village, FL)

My baskets explore form, line, texture, and reflect my environment. Using primarily native Florida grape vine harvested at a local preserve, I construct basketry forms using both traditional and non-traditional interlacing techniques.

I am foremost a basketmaker and am drawn to the purity of the vessel shape, but I am equally attentive to its potential as a sculptural object.

I begin constructing by first sketching, but these are crude markings that are meant only to be beginning concepts that leave room for evolving ideas.

My pieces take shape slowly as I manipulate the linear elements into a form that expresses volume and hopefully creates visual impact.

Even as I prepare my thoughts on a new piece, I am ever mindful of the heritage of basketmaking. These objects were man's first vessels predating ceramics and were both functional yet highly evolved aesthetically. Understanding this, I seek my own personal interpretation of the form and continually challenge myself to make each piece express both containment and have sculptural integrity.

■ Basket #31, 2000
Florida native grape vine, reed,
stripped Florida native grape vine
21 x 17 x 20 inches

Merrill Morrison

(b. 1949, Syracuse, NY; lives in Beverly Hills, CA)

I have always loved beads and fibers. As a young girl, I would sift through my grandmother's boxes of beads and trinkets, separating the shapes and colors…spending hours just playing and arranging and creating "stuff." As I got older, my mother taught me embroidery and then knitting, and I lost myself in the process of creating with my hands. My love of fiber continued with tapestry weaving in the 1970s, and evolved with papermaking in the 1980s and then knotting in the 1990s. As soon as I learned to knot, I knew I was hooked. I loved the tactile feel of the waxed linen, as well as the rhythm of making the knots over and over until my shape took form. I incorporated beads into the second piece I made and have been using the two mediums together ever since.

I was trained as a graphic designer and I find that it is my greatest influence. Graphic elements and strong, contrasting colors are always found in my work. However, my inspirations range from the extraordinary colors found in nature to the beaded detail work on a magnificent couture evening gown…

On the most personal level, knotting gives me a chance to immerse myself in a very peaceful, private meditative process that allows me to create simple, elegant forms with bold, striking colors. The use of glass beads adds luster and texture.

I have recently started using Right Angle Bead Weaving in combination with the knotted waxed linen. This technique allows me a multitude of possibilities in surface embellishment as well as the ability to incorporate additional dimensions of layering.

■ Musical Chairs, 2001
waxed linen, Japanese glass beads
7 1/2 x 8 x 3 inches

᛫Judy Mulford

(b. 1938, Los Angeles, CA; lives in Carpinteria, CA)

I work with containers because they make me happy. Each piece I create becomes a container of conscious and unconscious thoughts and feelings: a nest, a womb, a secret, a surprise, or a giggle, and always, a feeling of being in touch with my female ancestral beginnings. My containers contain "me."

Being a wife, mother, and "Nana" have been the most important things in my life. My baskets honor and celebrate the family. I use images of women and children because I want my basket/vessels to have content, to say something. I want to validate the importance of the family and the values and morals it nurtures.

Throughout history women have found creative time in their lives to make baskets. Knotless netting, the technique I use to cover gourds and molded forms, is an ancient, tedious, continuous thread technique that is used for nets, baskets, and button holes and is symbolic of women's work in the home.

Mother and Child, 2001
gourd, waxed linen, fine silver, pearls,
beads, antique hat pins, polymer,
pounded tin can lids, fork, photo transfers,
sewing things, antique buttons, journal
14 1/2 x 8 1/2 x 5 1/2 inches

■ By the Sea, 2001
gourd, waxed linen, Carpinteria sand, fresh
and salt water pearls, photo transfers,
polymer, pounded tin can lids, beads, fine silver,
silver spoons, shells, journal, antique buttons
11 1/2 x 12 inches diameter

˙Leon Niehues

(b. 1951, Seneca, KS; lives in Huntsville, AR)

I use three materials in my baskets: white oak, coral berry runners, and waxed linen thread. The materials I work with are a limiting factor, but I like to work within constraints. When I begin a basket, it is form that I consider first. Throughout the process I am employing simple and direct techniques that can be built upon. I look at my baskets as constructions, and I build on them until the basket is complete. Most recently, my basket forms are becoming more fluid, allowing the work to "open-up" and become less rigid.

■ Chan Juan #63-2001, 2001
white oak, emery cloth, brass bolts
16 x 14 x 11 inches

Wan Zhi #64-2001, 2001
white oak, emery cloth, brass bolts
16 x 11 inches diameter

Bird Ross

(b. 1957, Fort Smith, AR; lives in Madison, WI)

Four airplanes (266), the confirmed dead (201), the 5,422 people still missing and those that died at the Pentagon (188) equals a little over 6,000. —as of today 6,077. I wanted to know what 6,000 looked like. How can anyone possibly imagine what 6,000 of anything look like, let alone people. What would 6,000 names struck from the pages of a phonebook look like? What would it look like in terms of their handprints, their footprints, in terms of the number of people that miss them? It's like nothing we can imagine. This was my attempt to imagine. —18 September 2001

■ What 6,000 Looks Like, 2001
lentils, split peas, scotch tape
11 x 14 inches diameter

˙Jane Sauer

(b. 1937, St. Louis, MO; lives in Santa Fe, NM)

I love the sense of building knot-by-knot and row-by-row. I think of the rows of knots as lines wrapping around a form, giving it movement, weight, and direction. I love making order from the chaos of hundreds of threads and thousands of knots. For me the repetitiveness of the process is rhythmic and meditative. The boundaries of form and color seem to be endless and each piece stimulates numerous ideas for the next piece. Yet the most essential element is always the potential of this technique and material to be used as a dialogue between the viewer and myself.

My shapes have become progressively simpler and more sculptural as I have become increasingly more interested in the message of my work and less self-conscious about the technical aspects of the making. I seek to create forms that speak to the viewer, and challenge or provoke thoughts or emotions. I use either subtle veils and washes of color or saturated hues to further project my concepts. I am intrigued by relationships, both global and personal. Many of my works consist of two or three parts placed in a specific relationship to each other. The empty space between each piece is as important as the positive space. I want the whole to be stronger than each part. I select shapes and gestures, which express circumstances, tensions, contradictions, and the interplay of relationships in life.

My most recent work explores the interface between inner and outer self. I am making work in which the interior, which has previously only alluded to, is visually assessable. I have been exploring concepts of exposure, transparency, reproduction, dependency, and regeneration. The meanings of these pieces are multi-layered. My challenge in these pieces, and all of my work, is to embed concepts, emotions, and ideas in material form.

■ Chamisa, 2001
waxed linen thread, pigment
22 x 16 x 17 inches

Cass Schorsch

(b. 1941, Sabetha, KS; lives in Ludington, MI)

The challenge and enjoyment in building natural bark baskets is receiving the gifts of the forest and blending them into useful and beautiful products. Finding what the materials tell you they want to do and seeing if you can fulfill these messages. My rewards are both working with these materials and teaching the discoveries and techniques to others.

During the past 15 years, my appreciation and respect for these materials of the forest has grown even deeper. My senses feel the flow from the woods to the baskets. I am happiest when harvesting and gathering my weaving materials in the spring. As you harvest from each individual tree, it tells you what happened during its lifetime, and it seems willing to have a beautiful legacy constructed to live on in the future. That legacy created is my reward as well as the viewer's feelings when they are able to see and feel the finished product, as I did during its inception.

■ Stairway to the Past, 2000
birch bark, copper, cedar, oak
12 5/8 x 11 x 4 inches

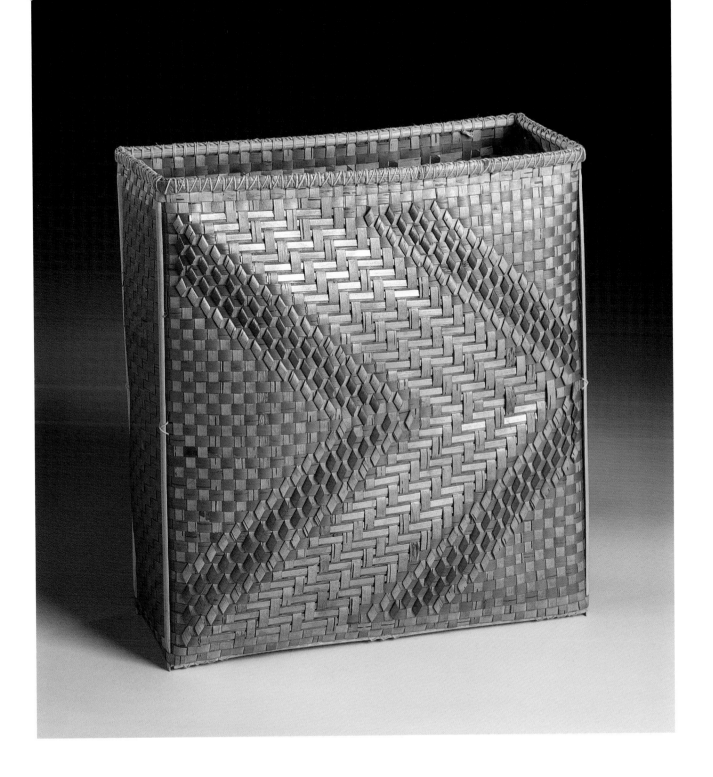

'Kay Sekimachi

(b. 1926, San Francisco, CA; lives in Berkeley, CA)

I have been making baskets/boxes on and off since 1975.

Techniques include weaving, folding, laminating, bonding and ply split braiding in linen, cotton cord, paper, undressed flax, and skeleton leaves. The two works in this exhibition are my most recent woven boxes in the series I call *Takarabakos*. I like to think that the meaning of the word *Takarabako*—strong, precious, treasure box—is appropriate.

■ Takarabako XI, 2001
linen, acrylic paint, bone
9 1/2 x 5 x 6 inches

Takarabako XII, 2001
linen, acrylic paint, bone
9 3/4 x 5 x 6 inches

Norman Sherfield

(b. 1948, Leavenworth, KS; lives in Sunland, CA)

I create small sculptures using a basketry technique known as knotting. It is a simple overhand knot that is knotted around a core of waxed linen threads. With variations of this simple knot, which is repeated over and over, I am able to create a variety of shapes, textures, and color patterning. The simplicity of the basic knot, combined with the repetitive nature of knotting, is meditative and allows me to immerse myself in the work. As each knot is tied, it is as though a pulse is added to the form, as though I am breathing life into the weave. The sculptures grow as I work on them, forming baskets or containers of potential life in symbolic form.

Two major influences running through my work are that of biological science and the automatism of surrealism. Natural biological form is alluring and fascinating to me, and defines the basis for my exploration of form. Building on the forms of the natural world, I combine instinctual and imaginative impulses with dream imagery to explore the boundaries where mind and nature meet. I feel my work is most successful when the viewer finds understanding of the piece in being intrigued with the unknowable. The content of the work is for the viewer to contemplate and complete; only becoming whole with the intellectual and spiritual contribution of the viewer.

■ Metamorphosis, 2000
knotted waxed linen, stones, found objects
9 1/2 x 3 x 3 1/2 inches

'Karyl Sisson

(b. 1948, Brooklyn, NY; Los Angeles, CA)

For years I have rummaged through garages, junk stores, and flea market stalls, salvaging cloth, buttons, and other sewing notions. I'm also drawn to women's vanity items like metal bobby pins, hairpins, and curlers. These common objects, suggesting domesticity and the feminine persona, are the inspiration for and often the very materials of my sculptures. I use objects that have a history and are familiar to my audience. The collecting, which I regard as a stimulating and worthwhile experience, is the first phase of a sometimes obsessive process of hunting, gathering, sorting, and connecting; where material, form, language, and meaning interconnect.

My basic structures develop by interlocking the materials; no glue, nails, or armatures are used. Interlocking is a common basketry technique. It maintains the integrity of the materials and creates patterning and texture intrinsic to the form. The artwork, like the process that creates it, is laden with patterning and repetition. Single wrapped twining, a technique I frequently use with zippers and twill tape, produces a different pattern and texture on the front and back sides of the form. The same is true of coiled tape measures. Since the tape is double sided, the exposed edge determines the interior and exterior patterning. In either case, inside could be outside, front could be back.

The study of inside/outside and how each conceals, reveals, or complements the other is referred to in my work. The basket or container form serves as a vehicle for exploring both formal issues (surface, space, shape) and personal ones (internal/external, open/closed, public/private). The tactile qualities of surfaces and the suggestive qualities of holes and cavities, coupled with the essence of the container and the idea of containment, present psychological themes of deep interest to me.

■ Double Bind, 2001
old cotton/rayon ribbon, thread, miniature
wood spring-operated clothespins
6 1/2 x 20 inches diameter

Heavy-Hearted, 2001
old rayon/ cotton ribbon, thread, miniature
wood spring-operated clothespins
10 x 16 x 23 inches

·John L. Skau

(b. 1953, Waukegan, IL; lives in Archdale, NC)

I think of myself as a sculptor/engineer/builder. My formal training is in fiber art. Contemporary basketry is my realm as I have worked with cloth as a pliable plane since 1993. I consider each of my contemporary basket forms as a sculptural object, each being an exuberant and assertive expression. My limited production works comprise numerous series of related forms such as the stre-e-e-etch basket, the cone, the bicorner, the tricorner, the planar, the bent plane, the swollen plane, and the swollen disk. This series of forms provides me the satisfying space to explore geometric pattern and rich color relationships, derived from woven structures, that I find so intriguing. No two works from these series are ever the same. The forms I create are elegant, minimal expressions having both a contemporary and timeless spirit.

In addition to these basket forms I also create sculptural objects that are not necessarily container forms. These works are often constructed using basketry techniques that are usually much larger in scale than the basket series. They are related to themes, prompted by my recent life experiences or my recent ethnographic studies. This body of work has evolved over the years. I may create two or three additional forms per year that I add to these sculptural series. Several have had titles like, "Snake in the Grass!", "I'll Build a Stairway to Paradise," and "Aztec Collection."

A significant part of the joy of my work comes with orchestrating the factors that comprise the basic elements. I start with thin strips of cherry, maple, or other hard woods with fine grains. I hand cut these strips to precise widths, lengths, and tapers, that once woven, create the attitude I seek. Often, I paint some of the strips as I consider the number required, select the weave structure, and plan the sequence of dark and light elements. The forms are seamlessly woven together using twill, satin, and double weave structures. The endless pattern motifs that articulate the surfaces of my work are a constant delight to work out. The forms are meticulously finished with bentwood laminations at the rims and edges and turned elements are often fabricated as bases for many of the baskets. All of my work is enhanced with a light application of varnish.

■ Horn of Plenty, 2001
maple, poplar, paint, varnish
32 x 17 1/2 inches diameter

Turn Right at the Next Corner, 2001
maple, poplar, paint, varnish, cherry
21 1/4 x 33 x 4 1/2 inches

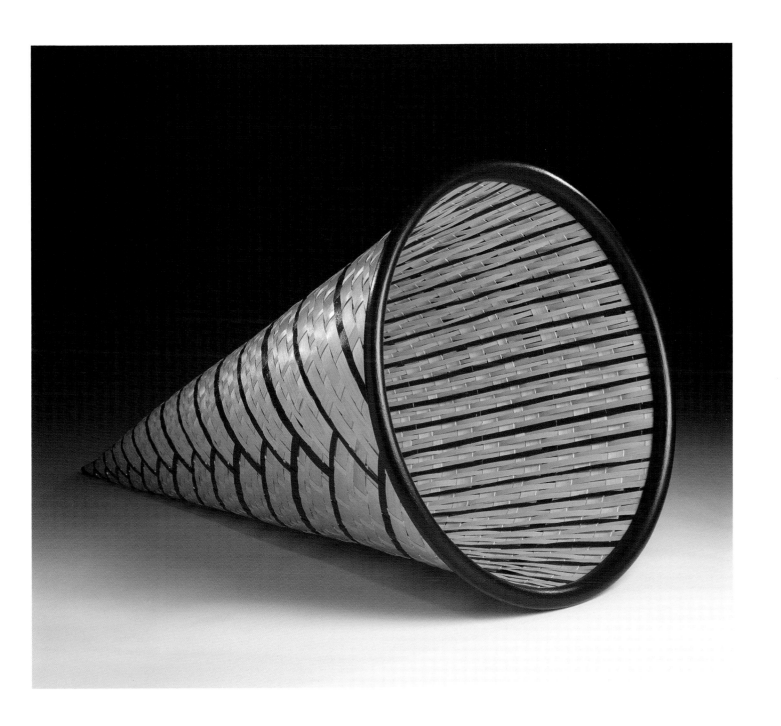

Leandra Spangler

(b. 1951, Lawrence, KS; lives in Columbia, MO)

Vessel is a metaphor for woman: container, receptacle, keeper, and protector. The role of Woman in a culture places her close to the hearth and children. It has been her responsibility to bear, nurture, feed, warm, clothe, cure, and protect her children. The basket, bag, or pot were woman's tools. They became symbolic of her importance to the survival of the community. After meeting the functional requirements for gathering, cooking, and storing, adding aesthetic variations to vessels was a natural progression. I, like her, decorate the vessels I create.

The twined reed vessels I weave are armatures for handmade paper. Traditionally paper is smooth, a surface prepared to receive expressions of the artist or writer. Graphite is a basic medium for artistic expression. Instead of making linear or tonal marks with graphite, I use it to enhance and define the surface quality of the handmade paper.

Using very ordinary artistic materials; 100% cotton paper, graphite, and reed, my artwork is unconventional and personally expressive. Simple in form, but intricate in surface, the vessels I create represent the universal qualities of woman: strength, complexity, mystery, and individuality.

Ten Thousand Wishes, 2001—What we aspire to, dream of, and hope for others are collections of our tiniest thoughts, expectations, aspirations, desires, recollections, and ambitions. These individual impulses collect, layer, and build into a powerful driving force, our passion.

■ Ten Thousand Wishes, 2001
reed, handmade paper, found paper, graphite
24 x 7 inches diameter
Steel stand fabricated by Don Asbee

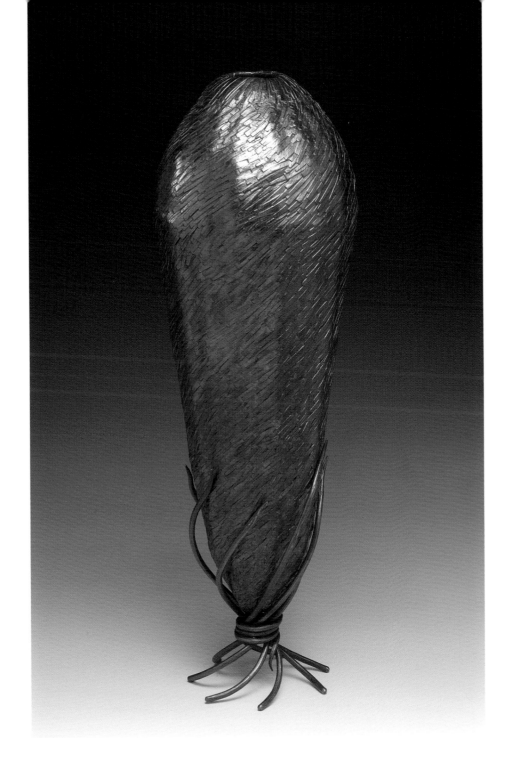

Jo Stealey

(b. 1950, Missouri; lives in Franklin, MO)

Coming from a background of ceramics and weaving, I learned to make paper almost 20 years ago. Influenced by all these media, I have always had a love for functional clay forms, as well as traditional textiles, particularly baskets. As a result, a vessel series was developed out of handmade paper, which has been the hallmark of my work for the past few years. These works represent recent experiments to expand my original concept of vessel in terms of content, imagery, form, and technique. More and more the vessel is a visual voice which reflects my reverence for ritual objects, ancient religious traditions, and what actually lies beyond the physical plane in which we live. Some of the works pay homage to the vessel itself. Others address metaphorical or spiritual ideas. Yet others, although conceived as vessels, move beyond the original form and take on new meaning.

Isabel Allende, a Chilean author, wrote a biographical novel entitled *House of Spirits*, the inspiration for this piece. In this book she weaves a story about a psychic grandmother, whose character is based on her own grandmother and the relationships of the grandmother, daughter, and granddaughter. The vessels represent the grandmother and granddaughter; the smaller vessel behind the larger vessel is the daughter. The house behind the bottom vessel is a talisman for the protection the women provided in the home. The "gate" at the top of the piece opens to reveal a scroll which contains secrets of the family and a young woman looking through a rock which alludes to a third eye. Allende, like many Latin authors, writes with aplomb in the style of magical realism which has been an allure as well as informed my life over the years. This piece pays homage to the inspiration she has provided me throughout her many books.

■ Spirit House: Nicho Allende, 2001
handmade flax paper, copper, mixed media
24 x 10 x 4 inches

Liz Stoehr

(b. 1954, Milwaukee, WI; lives in Avondale, GA)

My interest in constructing fiber forms originated in traditional basketmaking; following a pattern, measuring out lengths of materials, and feeling the sense of completion from matching the form with the "recipe." Gradually, I moved towards a freer style of construction remaining mindful of the rudiments of traditional basket forms. I am interested in constructing container forms that are organic, gestural, and textural. In addition to weaving the elements, I also utilize hand stitching techniques to build walls and then to connect these walls together. Container forms keep my interest because of the endless opportunities for construction and the infinite varieties of spaces that can be contained within these forms. I utilize both industrial-made and natural materials in order to construct baskets that reflect luminosity, texture, and scope.

■ Black Container #27, 2001
black braided elastic, thread, paper
25 x 7 x 8 inches
Private Collection

'Billy Ruth Sudduth

(b. 1945, Sewanee, TN; lives in Bakersville, NC)

My baskets blend the historical with the present through color, pattern, surface embellishment, and form. I am inspired by the classical shapes typical of Shaker and Appalachian baskets but I travel back over seven centuries for the most profound influence on my work: The Nature Sequence, developed by Leonardo of Pisa (Italy). Better known by his nickname, Fibonacci (circa 1170-1250), he was considered the most outstanding mathematician of the middle ages. The Nature Sequence, also known as Fibonacci Numbers, is written by starting with two 1's adding them to get 2, then adding the next two numbers successively: the first few terms being 1,1,2,3,5,8,13,21,34,55,89, etc. After the first few Fibonacci numbers, the ratios of any two progressing numbers approximate the Golden Mean (1:1.618 or 5:8), which has been used to unify design since ancient Greece. Because Fibonacci numbers approach infinity, the design possibilities are unlimited. The ratios are found in the spacing of the spirals on seashells, on pineapples, in the arrangement of the florets in the center of a daisy or sunflower, and in the curve of an elephant's tusk. Man has used the ratios in the shape of playing cards and window frames, on the piano keyboard and in the structure of great buildings. Farmers have used Fibonacci numbers to rotate their crops, stockbrokers have used them in investments, and computer engineers use them in computer programming. I use the Fibonacci numbers in my baskets. The rhythm of the pattern seems predetermined as if by nature itself.

Initially, I was concerned by my inability to free form, random weave, and become more expressive in expanding the possibility of a basket. However, the sense of order I gained by incorporating Fibonacci numbers in almost all of my work evolved into my "style," a natural progression of balancing a family with a career. As I have become more secure in my work, I have felt more comfortable with the order in what I do and it has become the basis for the direction in which I want to continue. I want to expand the possibilities of design while maintaining function. This object called a basket should look like a basket and not be so far removed from form and function that it is not discernible as a basket.

Seneca said that art imitates nature. Whether viewed as art or craft, my baskets demonstrate this. The weaving utilizes a mathematical structure of spiral growth found in nature to create baskets with a rhythmic, naturally flowing design. They are both visual and tactile, beckoning the viewer to touch and explore with the eyes and hands. I do not separate myself from nature but through my weaving, affirm being a part of it.

■ Fibonacci 19, 2000
twill, reverse twill, European cut reed splints, iron oxide and crushed walnut hull dye
14 1/2 x 19 inches diameter

Illusions, 2001
Japanese twill weave, European cut reed splints, iron oxide dye, acrylic paint
10 x 16 inches diameter

Gail Toma

(b. 1941, Honolulu, HI; lives in Honolulu, HI)

The Japanese warrior's helmet, the *Kabuto*, more than protects the head, it also serves as a mask, a disguise that transforms the wearer, and makes him larger than life. It announces his status as a samurai. During the later half of the 16th century and the beginning of the 17th century helmets of very individual designs known as *Kawari Kabuto* made its appearance. These fanciful helmets with their attached sculptural forms served to establish instant recognition for the wearer. The protective functions of the helmet were not neglected. These very distinctive helmets are examples of individual self-expression not commonly found in Japanese culture. In my *Kawari Kabuto* one can see the influences of my American-Japanese ancestry, materials from my Hawaii home and my love of basketmaking.

■ Helmet with Goat Skull and Horns II, 2001
rattan reed, goat skull with horns from Hawaii,
22K gold leaf, Japanese paper, abacca fiber, paint
27 x 24 x 22 inches (on stand)
Private Collection

Suzy Wahl

(b. 1940, St. Louis, MO; lives in Santa Fe, NM)

The idea of container with its interior space suggests to me the passions and turmoil within that are only alluded to on the exterior visible skin. Light shinning on and through the irregular surface lets my pictorial narratives have a more personal "telling" of the story. By using unmatched glass beads I can choose each individual bead for its particular variation of color, shape, size, and texture to make the "fabric" that is my canvas. Using a technique of netted beading gives my hands a controlled pleasure as I construct the vessel and a sense of "building" textured walls for each piece.

■ Whose Rainbow Are We Chasing, 2000
glass seed beads
6 1/2 x 4 1/2 inches diameter

Dawn Walden

(b. 1948, St. Ignace, MI; lives in Omak, WA)

An Ojibway descendant, basket weaver and carver, my education began at an early age working with and for Ojibway/Chippewa master weavers and carvers.

My traditional Great Lakes work has been greatly influenced in the last twenty years working with the tribes and weavers guilds of the Northwest. I received a great sense of natural form, craftsmanship, and attention to detail from Japanese-American weavers Jan Hopkins and Jiro Yonezawa.

My works' final crossing into Contemporary Art was bridged by workshops with John McQueen and much encouragement from friend and teacher Jan Hopkins.

My central focus for the past forty years has been preserving Native American basketry and technology. I have been teaching Great Lakes Native American Basketry for twenty-five years.

■ What is the Point, 2001
cedar bark, cedar roots, black ash, sweetgrass
20 x 12 inches diameter

Selected Biographic Information

Jackie Abrams

Education
1970 B.S., Child Development, University of Massachusetts, Amherst
1973 M.Ed., Humanistic Education, University of Massachusetts, Amherst

Workshops with John McQueen, Dorothy Gill Barnes, Lissa Hunter, Michael James, Nick Cave, Tony Hughes, Masakatsu Hasegawa, Hisako Sekijima, Jane Sauer, Shereen LaPlantz, Bryant Holsenbeck, Christine Lamb, John Garrett, David Paul Bacharach, Judith Olney, Carol Hart, Dianne Stanton, Maggie Henton, Keiko Takeda, Marilyn Moore and Nancy Moore Bess.

Selected Exhibitions
2001 *National Summer Faculty Invitational*, Arrowmont School of Arts and Crafts, Gatlinburg, TN
American Craft Enterprises, Baltimore, MD
SOFA, New York and Chicago, Katie Gingrass Gallery, Milwaukee, WI
2000 *New Talent in Craft*, Charles A. Wustum Museum of Fine Arts, Racine, WI
Smithsonian Craft Show, Washington, DC
Philadelphia Museum of Art Craft Show, PA
American Craft Enterprises, Baltimore, MD
1999 *All Things Considered*, Handweavers Guild of America, Inc., Arrowmont School of Arts and Crafts, Gatlinburg, TN
Innovation – Baskets and Beyond, Firehouse Gallery, Damariscotta, ME
American Craft Enterprises, Baltimore, MD
SOFA, Chicago, Mobilia Gallery, Cambridge, MA
1998 *Green Mountain Visions*, The Works Gallery, Philadelphia, PA
Contemporary Baskets, The Gallery at the Philadelphia Museum of Art, PA
American Craft Enterprises, Baltimore, MD
American Craft Exposition, Evanston, IL
1997 Smithsonian Craft Show, Washington, DC
Philadelphia Museum of Art Craft Show, PA
American Craft Enterprises, Evanston, IL
American Craft Enterprises, Baltimore, MD
Fantastic Fibers, Yeiser Art Center, Paducah, KY

Selected Collections
Karen and Robert Duncan, Lincoln, NE
Barbara and George Korengold, Chevy Chase, MD
Jane Korman, Fort Washington, PA
Sandy and Norman Mitchell, Potomac, MD
Anne and Harry Wollman, Woodstock, VT

Darryl & Karen Arawjo

Education
1976 B.S., Environmental Education, Pennsylvania State University (Darryl)
1975 B.S., Kutztown State University (Karen)

Selected Exhibitions
2001 *Woven Constructions*, Craft Alliance, St. Louis, MO
2000 *Enhancements – Handcrafted Functional Objects*, Exhibits USA, Kansas City, traveling
Way Beyond 101 – Contemporary Baskets, Fitton Center for Creative Arts, Hamilton, OH
Small Expressions, Carnegie Visual and Performing Arts Center, Pittsburg, PA
SOFA, New York, Katie Gingrass Gallery, Milwaukee, WI
Contemporary Baskets, del Mano Gallery, Los Angeles, CA
Contemporary Baskets, Dane Gallery, Nantucket, MS
Distinctive Visions, Connell Gallery, Atlanta, GA
1999 *All Things Considered*, Handweavers Guild of America Inc., Arrowmont School of Arts and Crafts, Gatlinburg, TN
1998 *Arrowmont National Juried Exhibition*, Arrowmont School of Arts and Crafts, Gatlinburg, TN
1997 *Turned for Use*, San Antonio Museum of Art, TX

Dorothy Gill Barnes

Education
1951 M.A., University of Iowa, Iowa City
1949 B.A., University of Iowa, Iowa City
1949 Cranbrook Academy of Art, Bloomfield Hills, MI, summer

Selected Exhibitions
1999 *From the Woods: Works by Dorothy Gill Barnes*, Ohio Craft Museum, Columbus
1998 *Threads: Inventing America*, Barbican Centre, London, England
Five Points of View, San Francisco Craft & Folk Art Museum, CA
1997 *Art Baskets*, Ohio Craft Museum, Columbus

Selected Collections
Arkansas Arts Center, Little Rock, AR
Erie Museum of Art, PA
Renwick Gallery of the Smithsonian American Art Museum, Washington, DC
American Craft Museum, New York, NY
Schumacher Gallery Columbus OH
Christchurch Polytechnic, New Zealand

Nancy Moore Bess

Education
1967 B.A. in English, University of California-Davis, CA
Post Graduate Work: University of California-Davis, State University of New York at Stony Brook, Teachers College at Columbia University, New York, Fashion Institute of Technology New York and Craft Students League, New York

Selected Exhibitions
2001 *Japan: Under the Influence*, Brown/Grotta Gallery, Wilton, CT
Contemporary Baskets 2000, del Mano Gallery, Los Angeles, CA
25 Years of Fine Craftsmanship, Brookfield Craft Center, CT
Woven Construction, Craft Alliance, St. Louis, MO
2000 *The Nature of Fiber*, Stone Quarry Hill Art Park, Cazenovia, New York
Contemporary Baskets 2000, del Mano Gallery, Los Angeles, CA
The 7th International Shoe Box Sculpture Exhibition, University of Hawaii, Honolulu, HI
Inventions and Constructions: New Baskets, Florida Craftsman Gallery, St. Petersburg, FL
1999 *25 for 25th*, Brown/Grotta Gallery, Wilton, CT
The Japanese Aesthetic, R. Duane Reed Gallery, St. Louis, MO
1998 *9 x 9 x 3*, American Craft Museum, New York
12.Biennial of Minitextiles International, Szombathely, Hungary
Threads: Contemporary American Basketry, Barbican Centre, London, England
"In Our Hands" 4th International Competition, Nagoya, Japan
Woven Forms: Contemporary American Basketry, Haydon Gallery, Nebraska Art Association, Lincoln, NE
1997 *Contemporary Art Baskets, 1997*, Ohio Craft Museum, Columbus, OH
New Baskets: Expanding the Concept, Craft Alliance, St. Louis, MO
Invitational, Nancy Sachs Gallery, St. Louis, MO
International Textile Fair Competition, Kyoto, Japan

Selected Collections
American Craft Museum, New York, NY
Arkansas Arts Center, Little Rock, AR
Dorothy and George Saxe, San Francisco, CA
Jack Lenor Larsen, New York, NY
Camille J. and Alex Cook, Western Springs, IL
Erie Art Museum, PA
Szombathelyi Muzeum, Szombathely, Hungary
Charles A. Wustum Museum of Fine Arts, Racine, WI

Jerry Bleem

Education
1992 M.F.A., The School of the Art Institute of Chicago, IL
1982 M/Div., Catholic Theological Union at Chicago
1976 B.A., Quincy College, Quincy, IL

Selected Exhibitions
2001 *Abstraction: the Power of Memory*, Christians in the Visual Arts, traveling
Contemporary Baskets 2001, del Mano Gallery, Los Angeles, CA
New Forms in Fiber: Trends and Traditions, Mobilia Gallery, Cambridge, MA
Fiberart International 2001, Pittsburg Center for the Arts, PA
Surface-Structure-Substance, New Harmony Gallery of Contemporary Art, New Harmony, IN
2000 *Transit*, University Art Gallery, Hooper-Schaefer Fine Arts Center, Baylor University, Waco, TX
Inventions and Constructions: New Baskets, Florida Craftsmen, St. Petersburg, FL, traveling
Way Beyond 101, Contemporary Baskets, Fitton Center for Creative Arts, Hamilton, OH
National Summer Faculty Invitational, Arrowmont School for Arts and Crafts, Gatlinburg TN
Material Evidence, Reed Wipple Cultural Center, Las Vegas, NV, traveling
1999 *Magic and Ritual: Hanukkiahs through Contemporary Eyes*, Steinbaum Krauss Gallery, New York, NY
Men of Cloth, Loveland Museum/Gallery CO., traveling
Fantastic Fibers, Yeiser Art Center, Paducah, KY
Art of Home and Farm, Ohio State University Gallery, Newark, OH
Crafts National 33, Zoller Gallery, Pennsylvania State University

---

The Object of Sculpture, Wright State University Art galleries, Dayton, OH
1998 *Jerry Bleem: Something Inside of Me*, Roswell Museum and Art Center, NM
From Limb to Limb, Illinois State Museum, Lockport Gallery, traveling
Sculptural Fibers: The Next Generation, The Foster Gallery, University of Wisconsin, Eau Clare
In Flex / In Flux: An Annual Sculpture Exhibition, Chicago Chapter, School of The Art Institute of Chicago
Artifacts and Archetypes, Mobilia Gallery, Cambridge, MA
1997 *Ordinary/Extraordinary, Sculpture by Jerry Bleem*, St. Mary's College, Notre Dame, IN
Jerry Bleem Recent Work, Locus Gallery, St. Louis, MO
Fiberart International 97, Fiberarts Guild, Pittsburg Center for the Arts, PA

Joan Brink

Education
1967 B.A., Fine Arts, Connecticut College for Women, New London, CT
Apprenticed with Marvin Cohodas and Reggie Reid

Selected Exhibitions
2001 *Crafts from the land of Enchantment*, Craft Alliance, St. Louis, MO
SOFA, New York, Katie Gingrass Gallery, Milwaukee, WI
Contemporary Baskets 2001, del Mano Gallery, Los Angeles, CA
One-person show, LewAllen Contemporary, Santa Fe, NM
2000 *Indian Market Show*, LewAllen Contemporary, Santa Fe, NM
Pathways: Explorations in Native American Culture, Transamerica, Pyramid Lobby, San Francisco, CA
1999 One-person, LewAllen Contemporary, Santa Fe, NM
SOFA, Chicago, Katie Gingrass Gallery, Milwaukee, WI
1997 *Expanding Textile Concepts*, Nancy Sachs Gallery, St. Louis, MO
1996 SOFA, Miami, Okun Gallery, Santa Fe, NM

Selected Collections
Robert Redford
Diane and Sandy Besser, Santa Fe, NM
Lyn and Donald Hanberg
Stanley Marcus
Judy and Ray Dewey
Nancy and Robert Riley
Koerner Foundation

Deb Curtis

Education
1978 B.S. Michigan State University
1990 Teaching Certificate, Oregon State University

Selected Exhibitions
2001 *Fiber Celebrated 2001*, The Nora Eccles Harrison Museum of Art, Logan, UT
Celebration of American Basketry, Amana Arts Guild Center, IA
Basketry: A Cultural Bridge, Shermer Art Center, Phoenix, AZ
2000 *Empty Vessels*, Corvallis Art Center, OR
The Art of Basketry, Everett Center for the Arts, WA
1999 *All Things Considered*, Handweavers Guild of America, Inc., Arrowmont School for Arts and Crafts, Gatlinburg, TN
The Best of Oregon, Weaving Guild of Oregon, traveling
Fiber Celebrated '99, The Albuquerque Museum, Albuquerque, NM
Small Expressions, Handweavers Guild of America, Mississippi Museum of Art, Jackson
Basketry: A Cultural Bridge, Shermer Art Center, Phoenix, AZ
1998 *Aesthetics '98*, Birger Sandzen Gallery, Lindesborg, KS
Small Expressions, Handweavers Guild of America Inc., Atlanta International Museum of Art and Design, GA
1997 *The Artistry of Baskets*, Artlink Contemporary Art Gallery, Fort Wayne, IN
Traditional and Contemporary Basketry Redefined, Sunburst Gallery, Chelan, WA

Michael Davis

Education
1973-74 B.A., Painting and Ceramics, University of North Florida, Jacksonville
1972-73 A.A., Florida Junior College

Selected Exhibitions
2000 *Inventions & Constructions: New Baskets*, Florida Craftsmen Gallery, St. Petersburg, FL
Way Beyond 101: Contemporary Baskets, Fitton Center for Creative Arts, Hamilton, OH

Who Knows Where or When: Artists Interpret Geography & Time, Charles A. Wustum Museum of Fine Arts, Racine, WI
1999 *Contemporary International Basketmaking*, British Crafts Council Touring
American Basketmaking: Tradition & Innovation, Arrowmont School of Arts & Crafts, Gatlinburg, TN
1998 *Threads: Contemporary American Basketry*, Barbican Centre, London, England
Dressed in Colorful Dreams: Fiber, Furniture, Fabric, Connell Gallery, Atlanta, GA
By Heart and Hand: Collecting Southern Decorative Arts, Art Museum of West Virginia, Roanoke, VA
Modus Operandi: A Survey of Contemporary Fiber, Snyderman/Works Galleries, Philadelphia, PA
Woven Forms: Contemporary American Basketry, Hayden Gallery, Nebraska Art Association, Lincoln, NE
1997 *Beyond Function: S.E. Contemporary Crafts*, Columbus Museum, GA
Contemporary Art Baskets 1997, Ohio Craft Museum, Columbus, OH
SOFA, Chicago, Connell Gallery, Atlanta, GA
3 Person Fiber Exhibition, Vanderbilt University, Nashville, TN
New Baskets: Expanding the Concept, Craft Alliance, St. Louis, MO

Selected Collections
Arkansas Arts Center, Little Rock, AR
Orlando City Hall Collections, Orlando, FL
Renwick Gallery of the Smithsonian American Art Museum, Washington, DC
Charles A. Wustum Museum of Fine Arts, Racine, WI

Carol Eckert

Education
1967 B.S., Painting, Arizona State University, Tempe
Selected Exhibitions
2001 One-person, gallerymateria, Scottsdale, AZ
2000 *Inventions and Constructions: New Baskets*, Florida Craftsman Gallery, St. Petersburg, FL, traveling
SOFA Chicago, Snyderman/Works Gallery, Philadelphia, PA
Distinguished Works by Inventive Minds, LewAllen Gallery, Santa Fe, NM
Surface-Strength-Structure: Pertaining to Line, Snyderman/Works Galleries, Philadelphia, PA
SOFA, New York, gallerymateria, Scottsdale, AZ
1999 *The Art of Craft: Contemporary Works from the Saxe Collection*, M.H. de Young Memorial Museum, San Francisco, CA
American Basketmaking: Tradition and Innovation, Arrowmont School of Arts and Crafts, Gatlinburg, TN
SOFA, New York, Snyderman/Works Gallery, Philadelphia, PA
Carol Eckert/Fern Jacobs, Sybaris Gallery, Royal Oak, MI
1998 *Modus Operandi: A Survey of Contemporary Fiber*, Snyderman/Works Gallery, Philadelphia
Artifacts and Archetypes, Mobilia Gallery, Cambridge, MA
Sculptural Fibers: The Next Generation, Foster Gallery, University of Wisconsin, Eau Claire
Woven Forms: Contemporary American Basketry, Hayden Gallery, Nebraska Art Association, Lincoln, NE
Basketry IV, Joanne Rapp/The Hand and The Spirit Gallery, Scottsdale, AZ
Figurative Fiber, Connell Gallery, Atlanta, GA
1997 *Eighth Annual Basketry Invitational*, Sybaris Gallery, Royal Oak, MI
Food, Glorious Food: Artists and Eating, Charles A. Wustum Museum of Fine Arts, Racine, WI
Just Add Water, Joanne Rapp/The Hand and The Spirit, Scottsdale, AZ
New Baskets: Expanding the Concept, Craft Alliance, St. Louis, MO

Selected Collections
Mint Museum of Craft + Design, Charlotte, NC
M.H. de Young Memorial Museum, San Francisco, CA
Renwick Gallery of the Smithsonian American Art Museum, Washington, DC
Szombathelyi Képtár, Szombathely, Hungary
Charles A. Wustum Museum of Fine Arts, Racine, WI

Kathey Ervin

Education
1983 M.F.A., Ceramics, University of Illinois at Champaign-Urbana, IL
1981 B.F.A., Ceramic Art, Kansas City Art Institute, MO
1972-74 Peninsula College, Port Angeles, WA
Additional study: Basketmakers Weekend at Olympic Park Institute, Kent State University and Blossom Festival for the Arts

Selected Exhibitions
2001 *Festival of American Basketry*, Amana Arts Guild Center, IA
2000 *The Garden Art Show*, Arts Council of Snohomish County, Everett, WA
1999 *Together Again for the First Time*, Maple Grove Gallery, WI
All Things Considered, Handweavers Guild of America, Inc., Arrowmont School of Arts and Crafts, Gatlinburg, TN
1998 *The Uncommon Basket*, ArtsWest, Seattle, WA

Jacquie R. Fort

Education
Athens College, Athens, AL
1990 A.S. Interior Design, Indian River Community College, FL
Selected Exhibitions
2001 *Woven Forms: Explorations by Six Florida Artists*, Polk Museum of Art, Lakeland, FL
Solo Exhibition, Gallery Five, Tequesta, FL
2000 Beyond the Fringe, Florida Fiber Art, traveling
All Florida, Boca Raton Museum of Art, FL
47th Florida Craftsmen Exhibition, The Arts Center, St. Petersburg, FL
Four-County Juried Art Show, A.E. Backus Gallery and Museum, Ft. Pierce, FL
Art by the Sea, Center for the Arts/Vero Beach Art Club, Vero Beach, FL
1999 *Combined Talents: Florida National*, Florida State Museum of Fine Arts Tallahassee, FL
48th Annual All Florida Juried Competition and Exhibition, Boca Raton Museum of Art, FL
46th Florida Craftsmen Exhibition, LeMoyne Art Center, Tallahassee, FL
Art by the Sea, Center for the Arts, Vero Beach, FL
1998 *Group Exhibition*, A.E. Backus Gallery and Museum, Ft. Pierce, FL
Members Juried Exhibition, Off Center Gallery, Vero Beach, FL
Florida Craftsmen Area 6 Exhibition, Harris House of Atlantic Center for the Arts, New Smyrna Beach, FL
45th Florida Craftsmen Exhibition, Art and Culture Center, Hollywood, FL, traveling
1997 *Florida Competitive*, Center for the Arts, Vero Beach, FL

John Garrett

Education
1976 M.A., University of California, Los Angeles
1972 B.A., Claremont McKenna College, Claremont, CA
Selected Exhibitions
1998 *9th International Triennial of Tapestry*, Central Museum of Textiles, Lodz, Poland
1997 *Trashformations: Recycled Materials in American Art and Design*, Whatcom Museum, Bellingham, WA

Selected Collections
Albuquerque Museum, Albuquerque, NM
American Craft Museum, New York, NY
Arkansas Arts Center, Little Rock, AR
Philbrook Museum, Tulsa, OK
High Museum, Atlanta, GA
Oakland Museum of California, Oakland, CA
The Detroit Institute of Arts, Detroit, MI
Renwick Gallery of the Smithsonian American Art Museum, Washington, DC
The Minneapolis Institute of Arts, MN
Carnegie Museum of Art, Pittsburgh, PA

Mary Giles

Education
1966 B.S., Art Education, Mankato State University, MN
Workshops with Jane Sauer, Fern Jacobs, Dianne Itter, Lissa Hunter and Mary Lee Hu
Selected Exhibitions
2002 *Daphne Farago Collection*, Boston Museum of Fine Arts, MA
Solo Exhibition, R. Duane Reed Gallery, St. Louis, MO
2001 Mint Museum of Craft + Design, Charlotte, NC
10th International Triennial of Tapestry, Lodz, Poland
The Art of Contemporary Fiber: Carol Straus Collection, Museum of Fine Arts, Houston, TX
2000 Solo Exhibition, Mobilia Gallery, Cambridge, MA
Living with Form, The Horn Collection of Contemporary Craft, Arkansas Arts Center, Little Rock
1999 Solo Exhibition, R. Duane Reed Gallery, Chicago, IL
Contemporary Works from the Saxe Collection, M.H. de Young Memorial Museum, San Francisco, CA

Craft Council, London, England
Solo Exhibition, LewAllen Contemporary, Santa Fe, NM
1998 *A Celebration of American Basketry*, Barbican Center, London, England
1997 Solo Exhibition, R. Duane Reed Gallery, St. Louis, MO
Selected Collections
Erie Art Museum, PA
Detroit Institute of Arts, MI
Contemporary Art Museum, Honolulu, HI
Arkansas Arts Center, Little Rock
Fine Arts Museums of San Francisco, CA
Jack Lenor Larsen, New York, NY
Karen Johnson Boyd, Racine, WI
John and Robyn Horn, Little Rock, AR
Daphne Farago Collection, Little Compton , R I

Patti Hawkins

Education
1970 B.A., Psychology, East Carolina University, Greenville, NC
Selected Exhibitions
2001 *Celebration of American Basketry*, Amana Arts Guild Center, IO
Rock Island Fine Arts Exhibition, Augustana College, IL
2000 *Basketry Turning Points*, Handweavers Guild of America, Inc., Convergence, Cincinnati, OH
Indiana Basketmakers Association Exhibit, IN
1999 *Rock Island Fine Arts Exhibition*, Augustana College, IL
All Things Considered, Handweavers Guild of America, Inc., Arrowmont School of Arts and Crafts, Gatlinburg, TN
Association of Michigan Basketmakers Exhibit, MI

Jan Henry

Selected Exhibitions
2001 *Georgia Women Basketmakers; Their Baskets and Collections*
Small Impressions, Handweavers Guild of America, Inc., St. Louis Artist Guild, MO
The Celebration of American Basketry, Barbican, London, England
2000 *Spotlight 2000*, Southeast Craft Council Regional Exhibit
1999 *Innovation: Baskets and Beyond*, Firehouse Gallery, Danmariscotta, ME
All Things Considered, Tradition and Innovation, Handweavers Guild of America, Inc., Arrowmont School of Arts and Crafts, Gatlinburg, TN

Pat Hickman

Education
1977 M.A., Design/Textiles, University of California, Berkeley, CA
1962 B.A., University of Colorado, Boulder, CO
Selected Exhibitions
2000 SOFA, Chicago, Finer Things Gallery, Nashville, TN
Miniatures: 2000, The Museum of Art and Design, Helsinki, Finland
Collaboration with Lillian Elliott, Collection of the Pierre Pauli Association, Musée Arlaud, Lausanne, Switzerland
Miniatures: 2000, Helen Drutt, Philadelphia, PA
Surface-Strength-Structure: Pertaining to Line, Snyderman/Works Galleries, Philadelphia, PA
1999 *Artists of Hawaii '99*, Honolulu Academy of Arts, HI
Sculptures by the Sea, Bond, Sydney, Australia
Skin, University Gallery, University of Tasmania, Launceston, Australia
'99 Miniartextil, Como, Italy
Pat Hickman: Through the Gates, San Francisco Craft & Folk Art Museum, CA
1998 *Feast or Famine*, Kazuma International Gallery, Maui Arts and Cultural Center, HI
Fit To Be Tied: Artists Look at Weddings, Pegge Hopper Gallery, Honolulu, HI
First Annual Mixed Media Miniature Show, Koa Gallery, Kapiolani Community College, Honolulu, HI
Basketry IV, Joanne Rapp/The Hand and The Spirit Gallery, Scottsdale, AZ
1997 *Enduring Spirit*, Sybaris Gallery, Royal Oak, MI
50th Anniversary Traveling Collection Exhibition, Arrowmont School of Arts and Crafts, Gatlinburg, TN
New Baskets: Expanding the Concept, Craft Alliance, St. Louis, MO
The Fabric of Life: 150 Years of Northern California Fiber Art History, San Francisco State University, CA
4th International Shoebox Sculpture Exhibition, University of Hawaii Art Gallery, Honolulu, HI

Selected Collections
Renwick Gallery of the Smithsonian American Art Museum,
Washington, DC
Pierre Pauli Foundation, Lausanne, Switzerland
Savaria Muzeum, Szombathely, Hungary
The Wadsworth Atheneum, Hartford, CT
Arizona State University, Tempe, AZ
The Oakland Museum of California, CA
Arrowmont School of Arts and Crafts, Gatlinburg, TN
Arkansas Arts Center, Little Rock
American Craft Museum, New York, NY
The Contemporary Museum, Honolulu, HI

Patti Quinn Hill

Education
Asheville-Buncombe Technical College, North Carolina Basketmakers
Association Conferences, Association of Michigan Basketmakers
Conferences, Indiana Basketmakers Association conferences,
Handweavers Guild of America conferences, Stowe Basketry Festival,
and John. C. Campbell Folk School

Selected Exhibitions
2001   *Spotlight 2001*, American Craft Southeast Region, Arrowmont
School of Arts and Crafts, Gatlinburg, TN
Craft of the Carolina's, Ogden Museum of Southern Art,
New Orleans, LA
Craft Trails Artist Exhibition, Center for Craft, Creativity and
Design, University of North Carolina
A Celebration of American Basketry, Barbican, London, England
Focus Gallery at the Folk Art Center, Asheville, NC
2000   One Woman Show, Blue Spiral 1, Asheville, NC
Two for 2000, Blue Spiral 1, Asheville, NC
1999   *All Things Considered – Basketry Today*, Handweavers Guild
of America, Inc.,
Southeastern Basket Invitational, Blue Spiral 1, Asheville, NC
1997   *New to the Third Power*, Blue Spiral 1, Asheville, NC
Collections
B.F. Goodrich Corporation
First Charter Bank, Charlotte, NC

Jan Hopkins

Education
Workshops with Holly Churchill, Jiro Yonezawa and Anna Jefferson
Selected Exhibitions
2001   *Baskets – Tradition and Beyond*, Guild.com, an online exhibition,
Madison, WI
SOFA, New York and Chicago, Mobilia Gallery, Cambridge, MA
Seminal Works in Contemporary Basketry, The Fountainhead
Gallery, Seattle, WA
Woven Constructions, Craft Alliance, St. Louis, MO
New Forms in Fiber: Trends and Traditions, Mobilia Gallery,
Cambridge, MA
2000   *Basketry: Inside Out*, The Fountainhead Gallery, Seattle, WA
Basketry Turning Points: The Future Contains the Past,
Convergence 2000, Cincinnati, OH
American Handweavers: A Celebration of the Fiber Arts, The
Self Family Center, Hilton Head Island, SC
Sculpture and Fine Crafts, St. Louis, Artists' Guild, MO
Small Expressions 2000, Carnegie Visual and Performing Arts
Center, Covington, KY
1999   *Basketry: An Evolution of Form*, The Fountainhead Gallery,
Seattle, WA
All Things Considered, Handweavers Guild of America, Inc.,
Arrowmont School of Arts and Crafts, Gatlinburg, TN
Arrowmont National 99, Arrowmont School of Arts and Crafts,
Gatlinburg, TN

Selected Collections
American Cancer Society, Breast Cancer Network
Robert Fulghum, Seattle, WA
Bob Timberlake, Lexington, NC
Eric Barkan, Seattle, WA
Sarah and David Lieberman, AZ

Lissa Hunter

Selected Exhibitions
2001   Solo Exhibition, Nancy Margolis Gallery, New York, NY
2000   *The 7th International Shoebox Sculpture Exhibition*, University
of Hawaii, Honolulu, HI
Solo Exhibition, The Munson Gallery, Santa Fe, NM
Solo Exhibition, gallerymateria, Scottsdale, AZ
1999   *Fabric and Fiber '99*, Portland Museum of Art, Portland, ME
American Basketmaking: Tradition and Innovation, Arrowmont
School of Arts and Crafts, Gatlinburg, TN

Solo Exhibition, R. Duane Reed Gallery, St. Louis, MO
Solo Exhibition, The Sybaris Gallery, Royal Oak, MI
1998   *Modus Operandi: A Survey of Contemporary Fiber*,
The Works Gallery, Philadelphia, PA
Five Points of View: Baskets by Contemporary Artists,
San Francisco Craft & Folk Art Museum, CA
*Knot As They Seam: Puns and Permutations in the Fiber
Arts*, Maryland Art Place, Baltimore, MD
Solo Exhibition, The Munson Gallery, Santa Fe, NM
Solo Exhibition, Nancy Margolis Gallery, New York, NY
1997   Nancy Sachs Gallery, St. Louis, MO
New Baskets: Expanding the Concept, Craft Alliance,
St. Louis, MO
8th Annual Basketry Invitational, The Sybaris Gallery,
Royal Oak, MI

Selected Collections
Charles A. Wustum Museum of Fine Arts, Racine, WI
The Albuquerque Museum, Albuquerque, NM
Arkansas Arts Center, Little Rock, AR
American Craft Museum, New York, NY
Museum of Fine Arts, Boston, MA
The Kennedy School of Government, Harvard University,
Cambridge, MA
Sandy and Diane Besser Collection, Santa Fe, NM
Jack Lenor Larsen, New York, NY
Barbara Rose and Ed Okun, Santa Fe, NM
Dorothy and George Saxe, Palo Alto, CA

Kiyomi Iwata

Education
1967-68   Penland School of Craft, NC
Virginia Museum of Fine Arts, Richmond, VA
1970,73,76   Haystack Mountain School of Craft, Deer Isle, ME
1971,74-75   New School of Social Research, NY
Selected Exhibitions
2001   *Century of Design – Part Four 1975-2000*, The Metropolitan
Museum of Art, New York, NY
*The Art of Contemporary Fiber; Highlights from the Carol Straus
Collection*, The Museum of Fine Art, Houston, TX
2000   Solo Exhibition, Jan Weiner Gallery, Kansas City, MO
Art Textile Contemporain, La Fondation, Mary Toms-Pierre
Pauli, Lausanne, Switzerland
Defining Craft 1: Collecting for the New Millennium, American
Craft Museum, NY
Surface-Strength-Structure: Pertaining to Line,
Snyderman/Works Galleries, Philadelphia, PA
1999   *The Art of Craft*, Contemporary Works form the Saxe Collection,
M.H. de Young Memorial Museum, San Francisco
*Recent Acquisitions: Selected Additions to the Modern Design
Collection*, The Metropolitan Museum of Art, New York, NY
Baskets From the American Craft Museum, American Craft
Museum, New York, NY
1998   Solo Exhibition, Perimeter Gallery, Chicago
1997   *Celebrating American Craft*, Det Danske Kunstindustrimuseum,
Copenhagen, Denmark

Selected Collections
The Metropolitan Museum of Arts, New York, NY
American Craft Museum, New York, NY
Renwick Gallery of the Smithsonian American Art Museum,
Washington, DC
Fine Arts Museums of San Francisco, CA
Cleveland Museum of Art, OH
Georgia Museum of Art, Athens, GA
Rhode Island School of Design Museum of Art, Providence, RI
Charles A. Wustum Museum of Fine Arts, Racine, WI
La Fondation, Mary Toms-Pierre Pauli, Lausanne, Switzerland
Savaria Muzeum, Szombathely, Hungary

Mary Jackson

Education
1973   Trident Technical College, Charleston. SC
1963   Speed Writing Secretarial School, New York, NY
Selected Exhibitions
2001   *Naturally Baskets*, Connell Gallery, Atlanta, GA
Objects for Use: Handmade by Design, American Craft Museum,
New York, NY
2000   *The Renwick Invitational: Five Women in Craft*, Renwick
Gallery of the Smithsonian American Art Museum,
Washington, DC
Defining Craft, American Craft Museum, New York, NY
"ACE" Ashepo,Combahee and Edisto, Gibbes Museum of Art,
Charleston, SC

1999   *American Basketmaking: Tradition and Innovations*, Arrowmont
School for Arts and Crafts, Gatlinburg, TN
1997   *Mary Jackson Baskets*, Jefferson Bank, Philadelphia, PA
Selected Collections
American Craft Museum, New York, NY
Charles A. Wustum Museum of Fine Arts, Racine, WI
The White House Collection, Clinton Presidential Materials Project,
Little Rock, AR
Columbia Museum of Art, SC
McKissick Museum, Columbia, SC
Museum of African American History, Detroit, MI
Museum of Fine Arts, Boston, MA
Museum of the National Center of Afro-American Artists, Boston, MA
Philadelphia Museum of Art, Philadelphia, PA
Renwick Gallery of the Smithsonian American Art Museum,
Washington, DC

Ferne Jacobs

Education
1976   M.F.A., Claremont Graduate University, Claremont, CA
1970   Neda Ali-Hilali, University of California, Los Angles, Summer
1967,71   Olga de Amaral and Peter Collingwood, Haystack Mountain
School of Crafts, Deer Isle, ME, Summers
1964-65   Painting, Pratt Institute, New York, NY
1960-63   Layout and Design, Painting and Drawing, Art Center
College of Design, Los Angeles, CA

Selected Exhibitions
2000   *Made in California 1900 -2000*, Los Angeles County
Museum of Art, CA
Surface-Strength-Structure: Pertaining to Line,
Snyderman/Works Galleries, Philadelphia, PA
Miniatures 2000, Helen Drutt: Philadelphia, PA, traveling
1999   *The Art of Fiber: Contemporary Works from the Saxe Collection*,
M.H. de Young Memorial Museum, San Francisco, CA
One Person Exhibition, Sybaris Gallery, Royal Oak, MI
1998   *Ferne Jacobs, Selections 1995-1998*, Nancy Margolis Gallery,
New York, NY
1997   *Contemporary Art Baskets*, Ohio Craft Museum,
Columbus, OH
Selected Collections
Renwick Gallery of the Smithsonian American Art Museum,
Washington, DC
The Metropolitan Museum, New York, NY
The Mint Museum of Craft + Design, Charlotte, NC
American Craft Museum, New York, NY
Contemporary Museum, Honolulu, HI
The Detroit Institute of the Arts, MI
The Oakland Museum of California, CA
Rhode Island School of Design, Providence, RI
Royal Scottish Museum, Edinburgh, Scotland
Wadsworth Atheneum, Hartford, CT

Donna Kallner

Education
1980   B.A., Communications, Purdue University, West Lafayette, IN
Studied with Jo Campgell-Amsler, Joanna Schanz, Lissa Hunter,
Diane Stanton and Lee Dalby
Selected Exhibitions
2001   *Celebration of American Basketry*, Amana Arts Guild Center, IA
2000   Group Exhibition, Birch Wood Gallery, Lakewood, WI
1900   Group Exhibition, Birch Wood Gallery, Lakewood, WI
Selected Collections
Sarah McEneany, Milwaukee, WI
Barbara Grainger, Raleigh, NC

Donna Kaplan

Education
1977-78   Factory of Visual Arts, Seattle, WA
1970-72   B.S., Occupational Therapy, University of Puget Sound,
Tacoma, WA
1961-64   A.S. Professional Nursing, Chaffey College, Alta Loma, CA
Selected Exhibitions
2001   SOFA, Chicago, Katie Gingrass Gallery, Milwaukee, WI
Woven Constructions, Craft Alliance, St. Louis, MO
SOFA, New York, Katie Gingrass Gallery, Milwaukee, WI
2000   *Absolutely Beads 2000*, Beads and Beyond, Bellevue, WA
SOFA, Chicago, Katie Gingrass Gallery, Milwaukee, WI
Basketry: Inside Out, The Fountainhead Gallery, Seattle, WA
To Bead or Not To Bead, This Is Not The Question,
Galleria el Jardin, Santa Fe, NM

1999 *All Things Considered*, Handweavers Guild of America, Inc.,
Arrowmont School of Arts and Crafts, Gatlinburg, TN
1997 *Pure Vision – American Bead Artists*, Louisiana State University,
Baton Rouge, LA, touring

Selected Collections
Edmonds Art Festival Museum, WA

Susan Kavicky

Education
Self-taught
1994-97   Martha Wetherbee, Sanbornton, NH: Teacher Training
Level I-III
1992   Basket Techniques, University of Wisconsin – Superior
1989   Native American Crafts, University of Wisconsin – Superior
1988-89   Basket Weaving Classes, The Fine Line, St. Charles, IL
1986-87   Creativalidity I & II, Pam Elish, Naperville, IL

Selected Exhibitions
2001   SOFA, New York, Katie Gingrass Gallery, Milwaukee, WI
Juried Visual Arts Exhibition, Three Rivers Arts Festival,
Pittsburgh, PA
Festival of American Basketry, Amana Arts Guild Center, IA
23rd Annual Contemporary Crafts, Mesa Arts Center,
Mesa, AZ
*Hand Crafted: A Juried Exhibition of Ceramics-Fiber-Glass-
Metal-Wood*, Rocky Mount Arts Center, NC
2000   *Crafts Forms 2000*, Wayne, PA
SOFA, Chicago, Katie Gingrass Gallery, Milwaukee, WI
Sculpture & Fine Crafts, St. Louis Artists Guild, St. Louis, MO
1999   *Over & Under*, Old Court House Arts Center, Woodstock, IL
All Things Considered, Handweavers Guild of America, Inc.,
Arrowmont School of Arts and Crafts, Gatlinburg, TN
1998   North Carolina Basketry Association Convention

Selected Collections
Roger Ford
Marge and Dominic Minervini

Gyöngy Laky

Education
1971   M.A., University of California, Berkeley, CA
1970   B.A., University of California, Berkeley, CA
1971-72   University of California Professional Studies in India Program

Selected Exhibitions
2001   *Gyöngy Laky*, Nancy Margolis Gallery, New York, NY
Gyöngy Laky: Recent Work, MX Gallery, Barcelona, Spain,
Crossover, Art Gallery, Bury St. Edmunds, England, traveling
2000   *Inventions & Constructions: New Baskets*, Florida Craftsmen
Gallery, St. Petersburg, FL,
Surface-Strength-Structure: Pertaining to Line,
Snyderman/Works Galleries, Philadelphia, PA,
Second Mini International Contemporary Art Exhibition, MX
Space, Barcelona, Spain
Nature Re-Bound, Palo Alto Art Center, CA
Kunst in der Landschaft, Prigglitz, Austria
1999   *Material Witness: Masters of California Crafts*, Crocker Art
Museum, Sacramento, CA
Gyöngy Laky, Danske Kunsthandvaerkere Copenhagen,
Denmark
American Basketmaking: Tradition & Innovation, Arrowmont
School of Arts and Crafts, Gatlinburg, TN
Gyöngy Laky: Sculpture form Organic Sources, University of
California – Davis, CA
Contemporary International Basketmaking, Crafts Council and
The Whitworth Art Gallery, England, traveling

Selected Collections
Charles A. Wustum Museum of Fine Arts, Racine, WI
Renwick Gallery of the Smithsonian American Art Museum,
Washington DC
Philadelphia Museum of Art, PA
Arkansas Arts Center, Little Rock, AR
American Craft Museum, New York, NY
Monterey Peninsula Museum of Art, Monterey, CA
The Oakland Museum of California, CA
San Francisco Museum of Modern Art, CA
Savaria Muzeum, Szombathely, Hungary

Patti Lechmann

Education
1975   M.F.A., Ceramics, Michigan State University, East Lancing
1971-72   Post Graduate Work, Textile Design, Indiana University,
Bloomington
1971   M.S., Design-Housing, Department of Home Economics,
Indiana University, Bloomington
1967   B.S. Home Economics and Related Arts, University of
Georgia, Athens

Selected Exhibitions
2001   *Baskets: Tradition and Beyond*, Guild.com
2000   *Who Knows Where or When: Artists Interpret Time and Place*,
Charles A. Wustum Museum of Fine Arts, Racine, WI
Miniatures: 2000, Museum of Art and Design, Helsinki, Finland
Living with Form: The Horn Collection of Contemporary Crafts,
Arkansas Arts Center, Little Rock, AR
Miniatures: 2000, Helen Drutt: Philadelphia, PA
Surface-Strength-Structure: Pertaining to Line,
Snyderman/Works Gallery, Philadelphia, PA
1999   *Albers Gallery 15th Anniversary Show*, Memphis, TN
The Art of Craft: Contemporary Works from the Saxe Collection,
M.H. de Young Memorial Museum, San Francisco, CA
Contemporary Baskets '99, del Mano Gallery, Los Angeles, CA
Baskets and Beyond, Firehouse Gallery, Bristol, ME
American Basket-Making: Tradition and Innovation, Arrowmont
School of Arts and Crafts, Gatlinburg, TN
1998   *12th International Biennial of Miniature Textiles*, Szombathely,
Hungary
Celebrating Tennessee Women Artists, Tennessee State
Museum, Nashville, TN
American Basketry: Other Places, Other Times, Brookfield Craft
Center, Brookfield, CT
Vessel Show Invitational, Roberts Wesleyan College, Rochester,
NY
Woven Forms: Contemporary American Basketry, Haydon
Gallery, Nebraska Art Association, Lincoln, NE
1997   *8th Annual Basketry Invitational*, Sybaris Gallery, Royal Oak, MI
Basket Invitational, Nancy Sachs Gallery, St. Louis, MO
New Baskets, Expanding the Concepts, Craft Alliance,
St. Louis, MO

Selected Collections
Charles A. Wustum Museum of Fine Arts, Racine, WI
M.H. de Young Memorial Museum of Art, San Francisco, CA
Tennessee State Museum, Nashville, TN
The Metropolitan Museum of Art, New York, NY
Fine Arts Museum of the South, Mobile, AL
Arkansas Arts Center, Little Rock, AR
Cleveland Museum, Cleveland, OH

Kari Lønning

Education
Self taught

Selected Exhibitions
2001   *Objects for Use: Handmade by Design*, American Craft Museum,
New York
Diversity + Exploration: New Forms in Wood, R. Duane Reed
Gallery, St. Louis, MO
2000   *Who Knows Where or When: Art Interprets Geography & Time*,
Charles A.Wustum Museum of Fine Arts, Racine, WI
Scandinavian Artists, Brown/Grotta Arts, Wilton, CT
Living with Form: The Horn Collection of Contemporary Crafts,
Arkansas Arts Center, Little Rock, AR
1999   *Contemporary International Basketmaking*, Crafts Council,
London, traveling
American Basketmaking: Tradition and Innovation, Arrowmont
School for Arts and Crafts, Gatlinburg, TN
1998   *Four Contemporary Basket Artists*, Society for Arts & Crafts,
Boston, MA
FormKNOTfunction, The Society for Contemporary Crafts,
Pittsburg, PA
1997   *Contemporary Art Baskets*, Ohio Craft Museum, Columbus, OH
The Tenth Wave, New Baskets and Free Standing Sculpture,
Brown/Grotta Arts, Wilton, CT

Selected Collections
Renwick Gallery of the Smithsonian American Art Museum,
Washington, DC
Charles A. Wustum Museum of Fine Arts, Racine, WI
Mint Museum of Craft + Design, Charlotte, NC
Arkansas Arts Center, Little Rock, AR
The White House Collection of American Craft,
Clinton Presidential Materials Project, Little Rock
U.S. Embassy, Bangkok, Thailand

Dona Look

Education
1970   B.A., University of Wisconsin, Oshkosh

Selected Exhibitions
2000   Solo Show, Wisconsin Academy of Sciences, Arts and Letters,
Madison, WI.
Living with Form: The Horn Collection of Contemporary Crafts,
Arkansas Arts Center, Little Rock, AR
Nature RE-Bound, Palo Alto Art Center, CA.
1998   *Threads: Contemporary American Basketry*, Barbican Centre,
London, England
1997   *Celebrating American Craft*, Der Danske Kunstindustrimuseum,
Copenhagen, Denmark
New Baskets: Expanding the Concept, Craft Alliance,
St. Louis, MO
1995   *The White House Collection of American Crafts*, The White
House, Washington, DC

Selected Collections
The White House Collection of American Craft,
Clinton Presidential Materials Project, Little Rock, AR.
Philadelphia Museum of Art, PA
American Craft Museum, New York, NY
The Metropolitan Museum of Art, New York, NY
MCI Telecommunications Corporation, Washington, DC
Charles A. Wustum Museum of Fine Arts, Racine, WI
Erie Art Museum, PA

John McQueen

Education
1975   M.F.A., Tyler School of Art, Temple University,
Philadelphia, PA
1971   B.A., University of South Florida, Tampa
1964-65   Indiana University, Bloomington, Indiana
1961-63   Florida State University, Tallahassee

Selected Exhibitions
2000   *Comestibles*, Mobilia Gallery, Cambridge, MA
Identities Contemporary Portraiture, New Jersey Center for
Visual Art, Summit, NJ
Fretwork, Solo Exhibition, Elliott – Brown Gallery, Seattle, WA
New Work, Solo Exhibition, Nina Freudenheim Gallery, Buffalo,
NY
1999   *Weaving the World Art of Linear Construction*, Yokohama
Museum of Art, Yokohama, Japan
Positions of Fear, Solo Exhibition, Perimeter Gallery, Chicago, IL
1998   *Under Nut's Sky*, Buckham Gallery, Flint, MI
Celebrating American Craft, Den Danske Kunstindustrimuseum,
Copenhagen, Denmark
Threads, Visual Art Center of New Jersey, Summit, NJ
Structure & Image, Handworkshop Art Center, Richmond, VA
Installation, Haystack Mountain School of Crafts, Deer Isle, ME
1997   *Stairway to Heaven*, Installation, Fernwood Botanical Garden,
Buchanan, MI
Solo Exhibition, Garth Clark, New York, NY

Select Collections
American Craft Museum, New York, NY
Arizona State University Museum, Tempe, AZ
Arkansas Arts Center, Little Rock, AR
The Detroit Institute of Arts Detroit, MI
Nordenfjeldske Kunstindustrimuseum, Trondheim, Norway
The Minneapolis Institute of Arts, Minneapolis, MN
Mint Museum of Craft + Design, Charlotte, NC
Philadelphia Museum of Art, PA
Renwick Gallery of the Smithsonian American Art Museum,
Washington, DC
Charles A. Wustum Museum of Fine Arts, Racine, WI

Mary Merkel-Hess

Education
1983   M.F.A., Metalsmithing, Sculpture, and Art History, University
of Iowa, Iowa City, IA.
1981   M.A., Metalsmithing and Fiber, University of Iowa, Iowa City, IA
1976   B.F.A., Metalsmithing, Fiber, and Drawing, University of
Wisconsin-Milwaukee, WI.
1971   B.A., Philosophy, Sociology, and Psychology, Marquette
University, Milwaukee, WI

Exhibitions
2002   *Blurring the Line: Where Vessel and Sculpture Meet*, Craft
Alliance, St. Louis, MO
2001   *The Art of Contemporary Fiber*, Museum of Fine Art,
Houston, TX
Mary Merkel-Hess: Nature's Bounty, Philadelphia International
Airport, PA

Out of the Floating Waves, Minnesota Center for Book Arts,
Minneapolis, MN
The Art of Asian Paper, Cedar Rapids Museum of Art,
Cedar Rapids, IA
1999 *American Basketmaking: Tradition and Innovation*, Arrowmont
School of Arts and Crafts, Gatlinburg, TN
1998 *Threads: Contemporary American Basketry*, Barbican Centre,
London, England
Craft is a Verb, Mississippi Museum, Jackson, MS
1997 *Celebrating American Craft*, Den Danske Kunstindustrimuseum,
Copenhagen, Denmark
Ritual Vessel: Masterworks form the LongHouse Collections,
East Hampton, NY

Select Collections
The Metropolitan Museum of Art, New York, NY
American Craft Museum, New York, NY
LongHouse Reserve, East Hampton, NY
Philadelphia Museum of Art, PA
University of Iowa Museum of Art, Iowa City, IA
Charles A. Wustum Museum of Fine Art, Racine, WI

Sally Metcalf
Education
1972-3.5.6 B.F.A., California College of Arts and Crafts, Oakland
1971 Chapman College, World Campus Afloat
1968-71 Commercial Art & Design, Chouinard Art School,
Los Angeles, CA
Selected Exhibitions
2001 *Contemporary Baskets*, del Mano Gallery, Los Angeles, CA
2000 *Contemporary Baskets*, del Mano Gallery, Los Angeles, CA
La Quinta Arts Festival, CA
Pacific Northwest Art Fair, Bellevue, WA
1999 American Craft Council Show, San Francisco, CA
Contemporary Baskets, del Mano Gallery, Los Angeles, CA
La Quinta Arts Festival, CA
Pacific Northwest Art Fair, Bellevue, WA
1998 Pacific Northwest Art Fair, Bellevue, WA
Salem Art Fair and Festival, OR

C.A. Michel
Education
1983 University of California, Los Angeles, M.A. Art
1981 California State University, Fullerton, B.A. Art
Selected Exhibitions
2000 Solo Exhibition, Foster White Gallery, Kirkland, WA
Lacy Primitive and Fine Arts Gallery, Los Angeles, CA
Group Show, Foster White Gallery, Seattle, WA
1999 Group Show, Foster White Gallery, Seattle, WA
SOFA, Chicago, Snyderman/Works Galleries, Philadelphia, PA
Small Expressions, Mississippi Museum of Art, Jackson, MS
1998 *Survey of Contemporary Fiber*, Snyderman/Works Galleries,
Philadelphia, PA
Shoes as Muse, Pratt Fine Arts Center, Seattle, WA
Smithsonian Craft Show, Smithsonian National Museum,
Washington, DC
Woven Forms: Contemporary American Basketry, Haydon
Gallery, Nebraska Art Association, Lincoln, NE
1997 *New Baskets: Expanding the Concept*, Craft Alliance,
St. Louis, MO
International Art Competition, Whatcom Museum or History
and Art, Bellingham, WA
Fiber Arts International, '97, Pittsburgh Center for the Arts,
Pittsburgh, PA
Expanded Textile Concepts, Craft Alliance, St. Louis, MO

Selected Collections
First Federal Savings Bank, Los Angeles, CA
The Women's Building, Los Angeles, CA
Oz Entertainment, Century City, CA
Carbro Film, Hollywood, California

Norma Minkowitz
Education
1958 Cooper Union Art School, New York, NY
Selected Exhibitions
2001 *Art in Embassies Program*, USDS, Ambassadorial Residence,
Lome Togo
2000 *The Woven Figure*, The Sybaris Gallery, Royal Oak, MI
The Nature of Fiber, Stone Quarry Hill Art Park, Cazenovia, NY
Miniatures 2000, Helen Drutt: Philadelphia, travel, Museum of
Art & Design, Helsinki, Finland
The 7th International Shoebox Sculpture Exhibition, University
of Hawaii Art Gallery, Honolulu, HI, tour

1999 *New Sculpture*, Bellas Artes Gallery, Santa Fe, NM
Weaving the World, Contemporary Art of Linear Construction,
Yokohama Museum of Art, Japan
Figure/Fetish, PMW Gallery, Stamford, CT
1998 *Modus Operandi, A Survey of Contemporary Fiber Art*,
Snyderman/Works Gallery, Philadelphia, PA
9th International Triennial of Tapestry, Lodz, Poland
SOFA, New York City, Bellas Artes Gallery, Santa Fe, NM
The Amazing World of Fiber Art, Wadsworth Atheneum,
Hartford, CT
Five Points of View, San Francisco Craft & Folk Art Museum,
San Francisco, CA
1997 *Hung Out to Dry*, Steinbaum Krauss Gallery, New York City

Selected Collections
The Metropolitan Museum of Art, New York, NY
Renwick Gallery of the Smithsonian American Art Museum,
Washington, DC
American Craft Museum, New York, NY
Charles A. Wustum Museum of Fine Arts, Racine, WI
Museum of Art, Rhode Island School of Design, RI
Arkansas Arts Center, Little Rock, AR
The Detroit Institute of Arts, Detroit, MI
Mint Museum of Craft + Design, Charlotte, NC
M.H. de Young Memorial Museum, San Francisco, CA
Kwang Ju Museum, Korea

Benjia Morgenstern
Education
1965 B.S., Russell Sage College, Troy, NY
1965 Post graduate work in art history, Scuola Vicenza, Italy
(Ohio Wesleyan University)

Continuing studies at Thousand Islands Craft School, NY; Parsons
School of Design, NY, Fashion Institute of Technology, NY; Skidmore
College, NY, Penland School of Arts, NC; University of Alaska, AK;
Haystack Mountain School of Crafts, ME and Arrowmont School of
Arts and Crafts, TN

Selected Exhibitions
2001 *Woven Forms: Explorations of Six Florida Artists*, Polk Museum
of Art, Lakeland, FL
2000 City of Miami Beach, Inaugural celebration of Second
Thursdays Art Events on Miami Beach, FL
*Our House and Gardens: Works inspired by the Museum and
Ground*, Ormond Memorial Art Museum, Ormond Beach, FL
Beyond the Fringe: Florida Fiber Art, traveling
Tactile Visionaries, Tampa International Airport, FL
47th Florida Craftsmen Exhibition, Fort Myers, FL, traveling
1999 *All Things Considered*, Handweavers Guild of America, Inc.,
Arrowmont School of Arts and Crafts, TN
46th Florida Craftsmen Exhibition, LeMoyne Art Center,
Tallahassee, FL
Craft for the Senses IV, Florida Craftsmen Gallery, St.
Petersburg, FL
1998 *45th Florida Craftsmen Exhibition*, Art & Culture Center of
Hollywood, Hollywood, FL, traveling
1997 *Florida Craftsmen Regional Exhibitions*, American Craft Council,
Museum of Fine Arts, St. Petersburg, FL , traveling

Selected Collections
Equitable Life Insurance Building, NYC
State of Florida, Very Special Arts Florida Collection
Daphne Farago, Key Biscayne, FL
Cher, Los Angeles, CA

Merrill Morrison
Education
1973 B.A., Graphic Art, Hofstra University, Hempstead, New York
Selected Exhibitions
2001 SOFA, NY, Mobilia Gallery, Cambridge, MA
Contemporary Baskets, del Mano Gallery, Los Angeles, CA
SOFA, Chicago, Mobilia Gallery, Cambridge, MA
Knot That Small, del Mano Gallery, Los Angeles, CA
New Forms in Fiber, Mobilia Gallery, Cambridge, MA
2000 *Beadwork in America 2000*, Lincoln, NE
Hot Tea! 2000, del Mano Gallery, Los Angeles, CA
SOFA, New York, Mobilia Gallery, Cambridge, MA
Contemporary Baskets 2000, del Mano Gallery, Los Angeles, CA
The Teapot Redefined, III, SOFA, Chicago, Mobilia Gallery,
Cambridge, MA

1999 *From Fiber to Form*, California State University, Channel
Islands, CA
SOFA, New York, Mobilia Gallery, Cambridge, MA
Contemporary Baskets '99, del Mano Gallery, Los Angeles, CA
The Teapot Redefined, II, SOFA, Chicago, Mobilia Gallery,
Cambridge, MA
1998 *Woven Forms: Contemporary American Basketry*, Haydon
Gallery, Nebraska Art Association, Lincoln, NE
9th Annual Basketry Invitational, Sybaris Gallery, Royal Oak, MI
Contemporary Baskets '98, del Mano Gallery, Los Angeles, CA
Why Knot?, Angel's Gate Cultural Center, San Pedro, CA
Joyce Scott & Friends, Mobilia Gallery, Cambridge, MA
1997 *New Baskets: Expanding the Concept*, Craft Alliance,
St. Louis, MO
SOFA, Chicago, Sybaris Gallery, Royal Oak, MI
8th Annual Basketry Invitational, Sybaris Gallery, Royal Oak, MI

Selected Collections
Joan Borinstein, Los Angeles, CA
Gloria and Sonny Kamm, Encino, CA
Dorothy and George Saxe, San Francisco, CA
Susan Stein Hauser and Daniel Greenberg, Los Angeles, CA

Judy Mulford
Education
1982 Monterey Institute of International Studies, CA
1980 M.A., Art, California State University Northridge, CA
1978 B.A., Art, California State University – Northridge, CA
Selected Exhibitions
2001 *Contemporary Baskets*, Mesa Contemporary Artist Gallery, AZ
Knot That Small, del Mano Gallery, Los Angeles, CA
New Forms in Fiber: Trends and Traditions, Mobilia Gallery,
Cambridge, MA
*Once Upon a Time: Artists Examine Fairy Tales, Legends and
Myths*, Charles A. Wustum Museum of Fine Arts, Racine, WI
Woven Constructions, Craft Alliance, St. Louis, MO
2000 *The Woven Figure*, Sybaris Gallery, Royal Oak, MI
Contemporary Baskets 2000, del Mano Gallery, Los Angeles, CA
Bye Bye, Textile Festival 2000, Utrecht, Holland, traveling
SOFA, New York, Brown/Grotta Gallery, Wilton, CT
1999 *The Teapot Redefined II*, SOFA, Chicago, Mobilia Gallery,
Cambridge, MA
The End is Near: Artists Look at the 20th Century, Charles
A. Wustum Museum of Fine Arts, Racine, WI
Innovations: Baskets and Beyond, Firehouse Gallery,
Danmariscotta, ME
Book Art, SOFA, New York, Mobilia Gallery, Cambridge, MA
Contemporary Baskets-99, del Mano Gallery, Los Angeles, CA
1998 *12th International Biennial of Miniature Textiles*, Szombathely,
Hungary
Contemporary Religious Fiber Art, SOFA, New York, Friends
of Fiber Art International
Woven Forms: Contemporary American Basketry, Haydon
Gallery, Nebraska Art Association, Lincoln, NE
Basketry: Other Places, Other Times, Brookfield Craft Center,
Brookfield, CT
Why Knot?, Angeles Gate, San Pedro, CA
1997 *The 10th Wave-New Baskets & Wall Art*, Brown/Grotta,
Gallery, Wilton, CT
Eighth Annual Basketry Invitational, Sybaris Gallery,
Royal Oak, MI
SOFA, Chicago, Sybaris Gallery, Royal Oak, MI
New Baskets: Expanding the Concept, Craft Alliance,
St. Louis, MO
Contemporary Baskets-97, del Mano Gallery, Los Angeles, CA

Selected Collections
Mint Museum of Craft + Design, Charlotte, NC
Renwick Gallery of the Smithsonian American Art Museum,
Washington, DC
Charles A. Wustum Museum of Fine Arts, Racine, WI
Arkansas Arts Center, Little Rock, AR
Rita and Don Newman

Leon Niehues
Education
University of Kansas, Lawrence
Selected Exhibitions
2001 *Two Perspectives in Form: The Basketry of Michael Davis and
Leon Niehues*, Atlanta International Museum, GA
Basketry Invitational, materiagallery, Scottsdale, AZ
2000 *That Was Then, This Is Now: A 35th Anniversary Retrospective*,
Craft Alliance, St. Louis, MO
Way Beyond 101: Contemporary Baskets, Fitton Center for
the Creative Arts, Hamilton, OH

1999 *American Basketmaking: Tradition and Innovation*, Handweavers
  Guild of America, Inc., Arrowmont School of Arts and Crafts,
  Gatlinburg, TN
  Contemporary International Basketmaking, London Crafts
  Council, London, England, traveling
  Arkansas Craftsman: Leon Niehues, Arkansas Arts Center,
  Little Rock, AR
1999 *Basketry Exhibition*, materiagallery/The Hand and The Spirit,
  Scottsdale, AZ
  Baskets, Beads and Bags, Greater Reston Arts Center, Reston,
  VA
1998 *Quality of Dimension*, Walton Arts Center, Fayetteville, AR
  Woven Forms: Contemporary American Basketry, Haydon
  Gallery, Nebraska Art Association, Lincoln NE
1997 *New Baskets: Expanding the Concept*, Craft Alliance,
  St. Louis, MO
  Contemporary Art Baskets '97, Ohio Craft Museum,
  Columbus, OH
  The 10th Wave: New Baskets & Freestanding Fiber Sculpture,
  Brown/Grotta Gallery, Wilton, CT

Selected Collections
Robyn and John Horn, Little Rock, AR
Charles A. Wustum Museum of Fine Arts, Racine, WI
The White House Collection of American Craft,
  Clinton Presidential Materials Project, Little Rock, AR
Arkansas Arts Center, Little Rock, AR
Hot Springs Art Museum, Hot Springs, AR

Bird Ross

Education
1992 M.F.A., University of Wisconsin, Madison, WI
1980 B.A., French, Tulane University, New Orleans, LA

Selected Exhibitions
2001 *Shoes*, Madison Children's Museum, WI
  Presenters Present, Yuma Symposium Gallery, AZ
2000 *Teapots Transformed*, SOFA, Chicago, Leslie Ferrin Gallery,
  Croton on Hudson, NY
  TTTTTTT too ours, The Project Room, Madison, WI
  Who Knows Where or When, Charles A. Wustum Museum
  of Fine Arts, Racine, WI
  In Our Hands, NHK Hall, Nagoya, Japan
1999 *Needle and Thread*, Wendy Cooper Gallery, Madison, WI
  Wisconsin Triennial, Madison Arts Center, Madison, WI
  Garbed: Extending the Body, Experiments in Clothing, Studio
  734, Madison, WI
  From Arlene to Zach, 28 Years of Penland's CORE Program,
  Penland Gallery, Penland, NC
1998 *Dress Up! Artists Address Clothing and Self Adornment*, Charles
  A. Wustum Museum of Fine Arts, Racine, WA
  The Magical World of Fiber Arts, Seippel Center for the Arts,
  Beaver Dam, WI
  Threads on the Edge, Gallery of Design, Madison, WI
  Fiber Invitational 1998, Barrington Area Arts Council Gallery,
  Barrington, IL
1997 *Basket Invitational*, Hoffman Gallery, Portland, OR
  Trashformations, Schneider Museum of Art, Ashland, OR

Selected Collections
Charles A. Wustum Museum of Fine Arts, Racine, WI
Open Chain Publishing, Tempe AZ
The White House Collection of American Craft,
  Clinton Presidential Materials Project, Little Rock, AR

Jane Sauer

Education
1976-78 Design, Leslie Laskey, Professor of Architecture,
  Washington University, St. Louis, MO
1959 B.F.A., Washington University, St. Louis, MO

Selected Exhibitions
2001 R. Duane Reed Gallery, St. Louis, MO
  University of Nebraska, Lincoln, NE
  Distinguished Works by Innovative Minds, LewAllen
  Contemporary, Santa Fe, NM
  Surface-Strength-Structure: Pertaining to Line,
  Snyderman/Works Galleries, Philadelphia, PA
2000 *Making a Difference: Fiber Sculpture by Jane Sauer*,
  Arkansas Arts Center, Little Rock
  R. Duane Reed Gallery , Chicago, IL
1999 *An Inaugural Gift: Mint Museum of Craft +Design*,
  Charlotte, NC
  The Art of Craft: Contemporary Works from the Saxe Collection,
  M.H. de Young Museum, San Francisco, CA
  High Fibre: Contemporary International Basketmaking, British
  Craft Council, Manchester, England & London, England

1998 *Threads: Contemporary American Basketry*, Barbican Centre,
  London, England
1997 R. Duane Reed Gallery, St. Louis, MO
  Ohio University Art Gallery, Athens, OH
  The City Series, Cedar Rapids Museum of Art, IA
  Threads: Fiber Art in the 90s, New Jersey Center for Visual
  Arts, Summit
  Celebrating American Craft, Det Danske Kunstindustrimuseum,
  Copenhagen, Denmark

Selected Collections
American Craft Museum, New York, NY
Arkansas Arts Center, Little Rock, AR
Cleveland Museum of Art, Cleveland, OH
The Detroit Institute of Arts, MI
Museum of Nanjing, China
Museum of Suwa, Japan
M.H. de Young Memorial Museum, San Francisco, CA
Mint Museum of Craft + Design, Charlotte, NC
Nordenfjeldske Kunstindustrimuseum, Trondheim, Norway
Philadelphia Museum of Art, PA

Cass Schorsch

Selected Exhibitions
2001 *Celebration of American Basketry*, Amana Art Guild Center, IA
  Small Expressions, Handweavers Guild of America, Inc.,
  St. Louis Artist Guild, MO
2000 *Heritage of Baskets*, Michigan State University, East Lancing, MI
  SOFA, Chicago, Katie Gingrass Gallery, Milwaukee, WI
1999 *Basketry, A Cultural Bridge*, Shemer Art Center, Phoenix, AZ
  Arrowmont School of Arts and Crafts, TN
  Baskets and Beyond, Firehouse Gallery, Danmariscotta, ME
  SOFA, Chicago, Katie Gingrass Gallery, Milwaukee, WI
1998 *American Basketry: Other Places, Other Times*, Brookfield
  Craft Center, CT

Selected Collections
Michigan State University Museum, East Lansing

Kay Sekimachi

Education
1946-59 California College of Arts and Crafts, Oakland, CA
1956 Haystack Mountain School of Crafts, Liberty, ME

Selected Exhibitions
2001 *Intimate Eye: Paper & Fiber Forms of Kay Sekimachi*, Mingei
  Museum of International World Folk Art, San Diego,
  California
  Expanding the Girth, Bampton, Oxfordshire, & Nehru Centre,
  London, England
  Japan: Under the Influence, Brown/Grotta Gallery, Wilton, CT
  *Leading the Way: Asian-American Artists of the Older
  Generation*, Barrington Center for the Arts, Gordon College,
  Wenham, MA
  Made in California, Los Angeles County Museum of Art, CA
2000 *The Woven Form: Carole Beadle & Kay Sekimachi*, Cabrillo
  College Gallery, Aptos, CA
  The Art of Craft: Contemporary Works from the Saxe Collection,
  M.H. de Young Memorial Museum, San Francisco, CA
  Far Out: Bay Area Design, 1967-1973, San Francisco Museum
  of Modern Art, CA
  Making Change: 100 Artists Interpret the Tzedakah Box,
  The Jewish Museum, San Francisco, CA
  Material Witness: Masters of California Crafts, Crocker Art
  Museum, Sacramento, CA
1999 *Books, Boxes & Bowls: Kay Sekimachi & Bob Stocksdale*,
  Brown/Grotta Gallery, Wilton, CT
  Views Inside & Outside of Hawaii, Studio 7 Gallery, Holualoa, HI
  Held & Let Go, California College of Arts & Crafts, Oakland,
  CA
1998 *Perfection in Form*, Sam Maloof, Kay Sekimachi, and Bob
  Stocksdale, del Mano Gallery, Los Angeles, CA
1997 *The Fabric Of Life: 150 Years of Northern California Fiber Art
  History*, San Francisco State University, CA

Selected Collections
The Metropolitan Museum of Art, New York, NY
Arkansas Arts Center, Little Rock, AR
American Crafts Museum, New York, NY
The Minneapolis Institute of Arts, MN
Musée des Arts Décoratifs, Paris, France
Oakland Museum of California, Oakland, CA
Renwick Gallery of the Smithsonian American Art Museum.
  Washington, DC
National Museum of Modern Art, Kyoto, Japan
Royal Scottish Museum, Edinburgh, Scotland
M.H. de Young Memorial Museum, San Francisco, CA

Norman D. Sherfield

Education
Workshops with Jane Sauer
Selected Exhibitions
2001 *Los Angeles Knotter's Collective*, Free Hand Gallery, Los
  Angeles, CA
  Twenty-Fourth Small Works, 80 Washington Square East
  Galleries; New York University, NY
  Figurative Suggestions: Woven, Knitted & Constructed Forms,
  Sybaris Gallery; Royal Oak, MI
2000 *Contemporary Baskets*, del Mano Gallery; Los Angeles, CA
  2nd Biennale du Lin, Fiber Art Synergy Association; Paris,
  France
  From Fiber to Form – the unexpected, Studio Channel Island
  Art Center; Camarillo, CA
  Variations of Thread: Miniatures, National Museum of Folk
  Arts and Traditions; Paris, France
  Contemporary International Basketmaking
1998 *Clockworks*, Center of Contemporary Arts, Universal City, MO
  Why Knot?, Angel's Gate Cultural Center; San Pedro, CA
1997 *USA Craft Today '97*; Silvermine Guild Arts Center, New
  Canaan, CT
  New Baskets: Expanding the Concept, Craft Alliance,
  St. Louis, MO
  1997 Los Angeles Juried Exhibition, Barnsdall Art Center,
  Los Angeles, CA
  Fiberart International '97, 15th Biennial Exhibition, Pittsburgh
  Center for the Arts, PA
  Fantastic Fibers, 10th Annual Invitational Fibers Exhibit,
  Yeiser Art Center; Paducah, KY

Selected Collections
Charles A. Wustum Museum of Fine Arts, Racine, WI
Dorothy and George Saxe Collection, San Francisco, CA
Gayle and Andrew Camden Collection, Grosse Pointe, MI
Ruth Greenberg Collection

Karyl Sisson

Education
1985 MFA University of California, Los Angeles, CA
1969 B.S., New York University, New York, NY

Selected Exhibitions
2001 *Emotion Pictures: An Exhibition of Orthopedics in Art*, Herbst
  International Exhibition Hall, San Francisco, CA, traveling
  Tevet to Av – Celebrating Contemporary Judaica, Gallery of
  Design, University of Wisconsin, Madison, WI
2000 *Living in the Moment*, Hebrew Union College, Jewish Institute
  of Religion, New York, NY
  Women's World: A Work in Progress, Brookfield Craft Center,
  Brookfield, CT
  RE-Generations, Los Angeles Craft & Folk Art Museum, CA
  Miniatures: 2000, Helen Drutt: Philadelphia, PA, traveling
  *Living With Form: The Horn Collection of Contemporary
  Crafts*, Arkansas Arts Center, Little Rock, AR
1999 *The Art of Craft*, M.H. de Young Memorial Museum, San
  Francisco, CA
  SOFA, New York, Brown/Grotta Gallery, Wilton, CT
  Contemporary International Basketmaking, Whitworth Art
  Gallery, Manchester, England, traveling
  American Basketmaking: Tradition and Beyond, Arrowmont
  School of Arts and Crafts, Gatlinburg, TN
  Making Change: 100 Artists Interpret the Tzedakah Box,
  The Jewish Museum, San Francisco, CA
1998 *Vessel: Form and Function*, Palos Verdes Art Center, Rancho
  Palos Verdes, CA
  Textiles of Scale from the Brown/Grotta Collection, Montclair
  State University, NJ
  Threads-Contemporary American Basketry, Barbican Centre,
  London, England
  Karyl Sisson, del Mano Gallery, Los Angeles, CA
  formKNOTfunction, Society for Contemporary Crafts,
  Pittsburgh, PA
1997 *Contemporary Art Baskets 1997*, Ohio Craft Museum,
  Columbus, OH
  New Baskets: Expanding the Concept, Craft Alliance,
  St. Louis, MO
  *Trashformations: Recycled Materials in Contemporary Art
  and Design*, Whatcom Museum, Bellingham, WA
  HELLO AGAIN! A New Wave of Recycled Art & Design,
  Oakland Museum of California, CA
  Threads: Fiber Art in the 90's, New Jersey Center for
  Visual Arts, Summit, NJ

Selected Collections
American Craft Museum, New York, NY
Arkansas Arts Center, Little Rock, AR
Brigham City Museum, UT
Buffalo State College, Buffalo, NY
Erie Art Museum, PA
Fine Arts Museums of San Francisco, CA
Renwick Gallery of the Smithsonian American Art Museum, Washington, DC
Charles A. Wustum Museum of Fine Arts, Racine, WI

John Skau
Education
1985   M.F.A., Cranbrook Academy of Art, Bloomfield Hills, MI
1982-83   Florida State University, Tallahassee, FL
1981   B.A., Fine Arts, Northern Illinois University, Dekalb, IL
Selected Exhibitions
2001   *Westchester Craft Show*, Westchester County Center, White Plains, NY
        SOFA, Chicago, Katie Gingrass Gallery, Milwaukee, WI
        Objects for Use: Hand Made By Design, American Craft Museum, New York, NY
        Woven Constructions, Craft Alliance, St. Louis, MO
        Smithsonian Craft Show 2001: Crafts for the Millennium, National Building Museum, Washington, DC
2000   *Winter Show*, Greenhill Center for North Carolina Art, Greensboro, NC
        Sculptural Basketry, The Society of Arts and Crafts, Boston, MA
        Transformation: Contemporary Works in Wood, Ohio Craft Museum, Columbus, OH
        Select 2000, Green Hill Center for North Carolina Art, Greensboro, NC
        Robert Lyon, John L. Skau and Suzanne Stryk, Blue Spiral I, Asheville, NC
1999   *Transformation: Contemporary Works in Wood*, The Society for Contemporary Crafts, Pittsburg, PA
        All Things Considered, Arrowmont School of Arts and Crafts, Gatlinburg, TN
        Non-Function: Objects for Contemplation, Penland School of Crafts, Penland, NC
        1999 Southeastern Basket Invitational, Blue Spiral I, Asheville, NC
        Agitating Utopia, Craft and Folk Art Museum, Los Angeles, CA
Selected Collections
Armstrong State College, Savannah, GA
ArtQuest Greenhill Center for North Carolina Art, Greensboro, NC
Charles A. Wustum Museum of Fine Arts, Racine,, WI
First Charter Bank, Charlotte, NC
North Carolina Center for the Advancement of Teaching
Redding Museum and Art Center, Redding, CA
Valencia Community College, Orlando, FL
Mr. & Mrs. James Goodnight, Cary, NC
Jack Lenor Larsen, LongHouse Reserve, East Hampton, NY
Media General, Inc., Richmond, VA

Leanda Spangler
Education
1981   M. Ed., Curriculum and Instruction, University of Missouri, Columbia, MO
1979   B.S. Art Education, University of Missouri, Columbia, MO
Workshops with Judy Mulford, John Garrett, Michael Davis, Lissa Hunter and Jane Sauer, among others.
Selected Exhibitions
2001   *Fiberart International*, Pittsburg Center, PA
        Woven Constructions, Craft Alliance, St. Louis, MO
        Small Expressions, Handweavers Guild of America, Inc., St. Louis Artists Guild, MO
        Instructor's View, Midwest Handweavers Conference, University of Illinois, Edwardsville, IL
2000   *On & Off The Wall*, Ponca City Art Association, OK
        Made in Missouri: Fine Craft by Missouri Artists, Craft Alliance, St. Louis, MO
        Missouri Fiber Artists, Missouri Fiber Artist, traveling
1999   *Scissors, Paper, Thread... Manipulated by Three*, Cityarts, Wichita, KS
        All Things Considered, Handweavers Guild of America, Inc., Arrowmont School of Arts and Crafts, Gatlinburg, TN
        Contemporary Crafts, Kirkland Art Center, Clinton, NY
        Wichita National 1999, Wichita Center for the Arts, KS
1998   *Material World, Spiritual Culture, A Fiber Invitational*, Brady Commons Gallery, University of Missouri, Columbia, MO

Surface New Form, New Function, Arrowmont School of Arts and Crafts, Gatlinburg, TN
Exploration: Tradition in Transition, Legacy Art and Book Arts, Columbia, MO
Woman: In the Broader Sense, St. Louis Artists' Guild, MO
1997   *2 x 2*, Davis Gallery, Stephens College, Columbia, MO
        Forming Connections: A Fiber Invitational, Legacy Art and Book Works, Inc, Columbia, MO
        Artistry of Baskets, Artlink, Inc., Contemporary Art Gallery, Fort Wayne, IN
        Fiber Art: National Contemporary Expression, Muse Gallery, Foundation for the Visual Arts, Philadelphia, PA
Selected Collections
Boone County National Bank, Columbia MO
Boone County Historical Society Museum, Columbia, MO
First National Bank, Columbia, MO
Hanna, Stanley, St. John Advertising Inc., Columbia, MO

Jo Stealey
Education
1992   Ph.D. Curriculum and Instruction, Art Education, University of Missouri-Columbia
Selected Exhibitions
2000   *From Here to Beyond*, Sioux City Art Center, IO
        Basketry Turning Points, Convergence 2000, Cincinnati, OH
        Paper/Fiber 22, Arts Iowa City, IO
        Woven Constructions, Craft Alliance, St. Louis, MO
        Textiles: Contemplative Language, University Center Art Gallery, Southern Illinois University, Edwardsville, IL
        Clay, Fiber, Paper, Glass, & Wood, Octagon Center for the Arts, Ames, IO
        Paper Works: On and Of Paper, University of West Florida, Pensacola, FL
1999   *Paperworks: Jo Stealey*, Walnut Street Gallery, Springfield, MO
        Jo Stealey, Rocheport Gallery, MO
        3rd Annual National Sculpture Exhibition, The Hoyt Institute of Fine Arts, New Castle, PA
        All Things Considered, Arrowmont School for Arts and Crafts, Gatlinburg, TN
1998   *Jo Stealey: Current Works in Cast Paper*, Emporia State University, KS
        Journeys, Passages and Portals, University of Nebraska, Lincoln, NE
        Theme and Variation, Southwest Missouri State University, Springfield,
        One Artist, Many Spirits, Maplewoods Community College, Kansas City, MO
        Paper/Fiber, XXI, Arts Iowa City, IO
        Material Wealth: The Beautiful Textile, Textile Center of Minnesota, College of St. Catherine, St. Paul, MN
1997   *Paint & Paper: Frank Stack and Jo Stealey*, Rocheport Gallery, MO
        For the Visual Arts: Solo Artist Series, Southwest Missouri State University – Springfield, MO
Selected Collections
First National Bank, Columbia, MO
May Foundation, St. Louis, MO
Museum of Art and Archeology, Columbia University, MO
University of Missouri – St. Louis

Liz Stoehr
Education
1994-96   Attended B.F.A. Program, Craft-Design, Fiber, Iowa State University, Ames, IA
Workshops with Mary Merkel-Hess, Dorothy Gill Barnes and Connie and Tom McColley
Selected Exhibitions
2000   *Basketry Turning Points*, Handweavers Guild of America, Inc., Convergence 2000, Cincinnati, OH
1999   *All Things Considered*, Handweavers Guild of America, Inc., Arrowmont School of Arts and Crafts, Gatlinburg, TN
1998   *Paper/Fiber XXI*, Arts Iowa City, IA
1997   *Art Show 9*, Hearst Center for the Arts, Cedar Falls, IA
        Paper/Fiber XX, Arts Iowa City

Billie Ruth Sudduth
Education
1975-88   Post Graduate studies in psychology, education, special education, learning disabilities and language, East Carolina University, University of Nevada-Las Vegas and Fresno Pacific College

1969   M.S.W., University of Alabama, Tuscaloosa, AL
1967   B.S. Psychology/Sociology, Huntington College, Montgomery, AL
Selected Exhibitions
2001   *Objects for Use: Handmade by Design*, American Craft Museum, New York, NY
        SOFA, New York and Chicago, Katie Gingrass Gallery, Milwaukee, WI
2000   *Smithsonian Craft Show*, Washington, DC
        SOFA, New York and Chicago, Katie Gingrass Gallery, Milwaukee, WI
1999   *Head Heart Hands*, American Craft Museum, New York, NY
        Southeastern Basket Invitational, Blue Spiral I, Asheville, NC
        Grand Opening, Mint Museum of Craft + Design, Charlotte, NC
        SOFA, New York and Chicago, Katie Gingrass Gallery, Milwaukee, WI
        Smithsonian Craft Show, Washington, DC
1998   *Craft is a Verb*, Mississippi Art Museum, Jackson, MI
        Billie Ruth Sudduth – Baskets, ERL Originals, Winston Salem, NC
1997   *The Renwick at 25 – The Reinstallation of the Permanent Collection*, Renwick Gallery of the Smithsonian American Art Museum, Washington, DC
        Celebrating American Craft, The Museum of Decorative Arts, Copenhagen, Denmark
Selected Collections
Renwick Gallery of the Smithsonian American Art Museum, Washington, DC
American Craft Museum, New York, NY
Mint Museum of Craft + Design, Charlotte, NC
American Embassy, Naimey, Niger, Africa
St. John's Museum of Art, Wilmington, NC
Glaxo Pharmaceuticals, Research Triangle Park, NC
Bank of America, Corporate Headquarters, Charlotte, NC

Gail M. Toma
Education
B.S., Art Education, University of Hawaii, Honolulu, Hawaii
Workshops with Lillian Elliott, Hisako Sekijima, Flo Hoppe, Michael Davis, Shereen LaPlantz, and Ed Rossbach
Selected Exhibitions
2001   *East is West in Hawaii*, Honolulu Academy of Arts, Honolulu, HI
1999   *Innovation – Baskets & Beyond*, The Firehouse Gallery, Damariscotta, ME
1998   *American Basketry: Other Places, Other Times*, Brookfield Craft Center, CT
Selected Collections
Honolulu Academy of Arts, HI
State of Hawaii Foundation on Culture and the Arts, HI
John Heiman, St. Louis, MO
Lawrence Takumi, Honolulu, HI
Dr. and Mrs. Benjamin Ichinose, Hillsborough, CA

Suzy Wahl
Education
1960   B.A., Art History, Washington, University, St. Louis, MO
Selected Exhibitions
2001   *Contemporary Baskets 2001*, del Mano Gallery, Los Angles, CA
        Woven Constructions, Craft Alliance, St. Louis, MO
2000   *del Mano Collaborative Show*, del Mano Gallery, Los Angles, CA
        Contemporary Baskets 2000, del Mano Gallery, Los Angeles, CA
        Beyond the Fringe, Lowe Art Museum, Coral Gables, FL
1999   *del Mano Collaborative Show*, del Mano Gallery, Los Angeles, CA
1997   *Contemporary Baskets '97*, del Mano Gallery, Los Angles, CA
Selected Collections
Dorothy and George Saxe, San Francisco, CA
Jane and Arthur Mason, Washington, DC
Fleur Bresler, Rockville, MD
Robyn and John Horn, Little Rock, AR

Dawn Walden
Education
Ferris State College, Michigan, Commercial Art Technology and Fine Art
Selected Exhibitions
Exhibited mostly in galleries in Oregon and Seattle.
2002   *Objects for Use: Handmade by Design*, American Craft Museum, New York, NY